# E X T R E M E
# W R I T I N G

## Discovering the Writer in Every Student

## Keen J. Babbage

Rowman & Littlefield Education
A division of
ROWMAN & LITTLEFIELD PUBLISHERS, INC.
Lanham • New York • Toronto • Plymouth, UK

Published by Rowman & Littlefield Education
A division of Rowman & Littlefield Publishers, Inc.
A wholly owned subsidiary of The Rowman & Littlefield Publishing Group, Inc.
4501 Forbes Boulevard, Suite 200, Lanham, Maryland 20706
http://www.rowmaneducation.com

Estover Road, Plymouth PL6 7PY, United Kingdom

British Library Cataloguing in Publication Information Available

**Library of Congress Cataloging-in-Publication Data**
Babbage, Keen J.
 Extreme writing : discovering the writer in every student / Keen J. Babbage.
   p. cm.
 Includes index.
 ISBN 978-1-60709-446-3 (cloth : alk. paper) — ISBN 978-1-60709-447-0
(pbk. : alk. paper) — ISBN 978-1-60709-448-7 (electronic)
 1. English language—Composition and exercises—Study and teaching
(Secondary) I. Title.
 LB1631.B195 2010
 808'.0420712—dc22

                                                          2009050290

∞™ The paper used in this publication meets the minimum requirements of
American National Standard for Information Sciences—Permanence of Paper
for Printed Library Materials, ANSI/NISO Z39.48-1992.

Printed in the United States of America

To the Henderson family—
Larry, Cindy, Kevin, Laura, and Mark

# CONTENTS

# ACKNOWLEDGMENTS

Life is short. Live your dream. Those two sentences are the best answer I can give to the question, "Why did you return to high school teaching after being a middle school assistant principal for 13 years?" The opportunity to live anew my dream of high school teaching became reality in August 2006. During the three school years since then, the joys of teaching have far surpassed the frustrations and the disappointments. The energizing experience of learning with my students has far surpassed the exhaustion that follows each week of 75 to 80 hours of work. I well recall that unique exhaustion from such weeks during my first year of high school teaching in 1980–1981.

My first expression of thanks is to the high school students I have taught during the years 2006 to 2009. Your achievements inspire me. Your ideas intrigue me. Your questions challenge me. Your answers to my questions confirm that learning is being caused. Your kind words of appreciation for my efforts are precious. Thank you for being the most important part of this teacher living his dream.

Several faculty colleagues provided insights about how they use writing projects in math and science classes. Many thanks to Dee Dee Hays, Becky Riley, Karen Gill, and Tammy Roark.

My maternal grandparents, Keen and Eunice Johnson, highly valued education. They set the standard, and they provided the resources. Decades ago my grandfather encouraged me when I told him my goal was to be a teacher. On the days when I live and work as honorably as my grandparents did, I have been in the promised land.

My parents, Bob and Judy Babbage, insisted that I excel during my years as a student. Learning was valued, reading was emphasized, knowledge of current events was required, and good grades were essential. I never matched my mother's straight-A result she attained during her four years at the University of Kentucky, but pursuing that standard multiplied my achievements in school.

My brother and sister-in-law, Bob and Laura, plus their children, Robert, Julie, and Brian, know that education is what life has assigned me, has called me to do. Their understanding of my dedication to that work is deeply appreciated.

During the past 15 years, I have been blessed with the opportunities to write 11 books about education. I write each original draft in longhand on notebook paper. Cindy Henderson then transforms those pages into properly word-processed text. The Henderson family members—Cindy, Larry, and their children Kevin, Laura, and Mark—have been very encouraging throughout these 15 years of creating books. For their friendship and encouragement, this book is dedicated to the Henderson family

Most of the people I know are people whom I met when they were middle school or high school students of mine. They range in age now from 45 to 16. They are forever in my memory, my heart, my soul, and my prayers. To those students, I say thank you for sharing part of your life with me so I could share my dream with you.

Keen Babbage
June 2009

# INTRODUCTION

There are two essential ingredients for writing: ideas and words. Writing depends upon an idea, a thought, some expression that will be communicated via words. Ideas and words are the vital signs of writing. Quality writing is a reflection of good ideas expressed effectively through precisely selected words.

Contrast these examples of ideas and words. Franklin Roosevelt wrote and then said, "The only thing we have to fear is fear itself." He did not write, "We probably can get along without being so afraid of stuff." It is written that Jesus Christ said, "I am the way, the truth, and the life." That is dramatically different from a written statement of "I'm a pretty good example that you could consider thinking about."

Ideas matter. The words that we select to express our ideas matter. The written expression of ideas through words can have extreme impact as shown in the following writings.

On Friday, June 5, 2009, the 2008–2009 school year ended in the school district where I teach U.S. history and political science to high school juniors and seniors. On that day there were two letters in my school mailbox. Examine the ideas and the written words in these two letters.

1. "I would like to thank you for interest in the associate principal position. We had many strong candidates, and the selection process

was a difficult one. We are not able to offer you a position at this time."

2. "Thank you for everything you did for me. I really enjoyed your class junior year. You are a great teacher. I honestly think I learned the most in your class than any other while in high school. I was never timid to answer a question when I didn't know an answer because you always found a way to relate an answer to what was correct. Thanks again, and I was really lucky to have you as a teacher."

The ideas communicated in these two written notes are powerful and are opposite. The style, the tone, the intention, the impact of those two written notes are the result of ideas and words. What is the impact of and the real message of each note? Is the first note a generic, bureaucratic, perfunctory completion of a tedious requirement? Could the first note have been written to build a bridge to future possibilities or did that note really intend to be a current rejection plus a permanent severance?

Is the second note a genuine, personal, sincere expression of kindness, appreciation, and encouragement? Does the second note show how words can express ideas that captivate and enhance? There is nothing generic or bureaucratic in the second note. Different ideas expressed with starkly different words that create opposite impacts thus show the potential power of ideas put into written words.

This book is about writing. Writing is about ideas and words. Ideas have no limits, yet also have no initial form or structure. Precisely selected words give the necessary form and structure to ideas so thoughts are transformed into designed written communication from which action can come. The purpose of writing is to put ideas into words. Finding and arranging the right words to properly construct an idea is the work of writing.

People talk much more than they write. Spoken words vastly outnumber written words. Most spoken words are applied in the moment to momentary tasks, duties, activities, adventures of life. Spoken words often emerge with an impromptu reflex as conversation or comments fill the silence.

Written words have the unique advantage of a structure, an organization, and a substance that combine to increase precision and impact. Writing can be revised, edited, transformed, deleted, modified. Spoken words can be improved or corrected only with more spoken words. That is one reason I give students this caution: "Not everything that comes into the brain should come out of the mouth."

What is extreme about *Extreme Writing*? This book applies fundamental concepts from *Extreme Teaching, Extreme Learning, Extreme Students*, and *Extreme Economics*. The essential concepts from those books are (1) learning is enhanced when connections are made between what students need to learn and the existing wholesome knowledge, interests, and talents that students bring with them to the classroom; (2) we know what works; and (3) the purpose of a school is to cause learning.

This book adds another fundamental concept to the extreme philosophy with specific reference to writing—students love to write and students hate to write. Building upon the factors that result in a love of writing can bring a powerfully productive dynamic into writing that students do for school.

High school juniors in the U.S. History classes wondered what we would do with our time after finishing the textbook and after taking a national exam in May with two or three weeks remaining in the school year. Our textbook concludes with chapter 42, but historical events continued after the book was printed, so the students wrote, designed, formatted, and created their version of chapter 43. The writing was impressive. The learning was significant. No two chapter 43 projects were identical, yet each was academically valid and each student knew the satisfaction of sophisticated historical thinking and of quality academic writing.

We have to move at a fast pace in U.S. History class to complete the study of people, events, and ideas since 1607. Interesting details about some topics must be omitted due to time limits.

The solution was a writing project. Our other project late in the school year was for each student to select one topic within U.S. history they would like to know much more about, do the research, write the findings and analysis, then make a presentation to the class. Their research was energized by the power of their wholesome interest in the topic they selected. Their writing was lively, meaningful, purposeful, filled with important information and sophisticated ideas. No student asked, "Why do we have to do this?" or "When will we ever need this?" Rather, an eager and sincere hope was expressed in the question, "Do we get to go back to the library today?"

We did spend more time than I originally planned in the library because the results with books, computers, topic choices, and research based on individual interest were superior. The students were learning, thinking, researching, and writing. The teacher was learning about how students learn.

The chapter 43 project and the "expertise project," which was what we called the select-your-topic research work, resulted in much learning, yet also resulted in much meaningful interaction. Students interacted with books, with ideas, with facts, with "I never knew that" revelations, and with knowledge. Students and I interacted as they shared with me their insights or questions, discoveries or problems. The projects enabled us to strengthen our classroom learning community and our commitment to and appreciation for each other; plus we completed the school year with very productive use of the concluding weeks, rather than coasting through days of pointless worksheets or videos.

Some writing assignments are primarily functional. "Copy these 15 terms from the board and then we will discuss the meaning and the importance of each term." That is similar to an athletic team completing some warm-up drills prior to a game or a musical group completing some warm-up notes prior to a concert. Warming up is important, but should be a temporary preparation for more significant action.

The basic functionality of some writing does not limit how the teacher can apply that writing task. "Now, before we discuss those 15 terms, put a check next to the term that you think is most important. Take a moment, and then we'll hear what term everyone chose and what your reasons were." That teacher began with a basic task that involved functional writing but was then built into a critical-thinking task that involves complex reasoning. No laws, policies, regulations, bureaucratic forms to fill out, meetings to attend, or other organizational procedures were needed.

What was needed? Some instructional design thinking, some creativity, an insistence on avoiding generic word-search wastes of time, eliminating busywork, and an awareness that students are real people living real lives right now, so the classroom cannot decline into the unreal, where the only reason to work is to avoid the punishments that come when work is not done.

Improved writing alone will not make every student a scholar, will not eliminate all high school dropout problems, will not guarantee a successful transition into middle school or into high school by each student, and will not quiet the endless complaints about educational achievement from politicians, community leaders or misleaders, or the media. Educational achievement is impacted by far too many variables for any one action to correct all substandard factors.

Of all the factors impacting educational achievement that educators can control, the factor that matters most is what teachers and students do in the classroom. If the classroom experience is right, education works. If the classroom experience is not right, nothing can compensate. Extreme writing is presented as one source of ideas and activities that can help make classrooms places where abundant, meaningful, real learning is caused.

Keen Babbage
Lexington, Kentucky
July 2009

nating busywork, and an awareness that students are real people living real lives right now, so the classroom cannot decline into the unreal, where the only reason to work is to avoid the punishments that come when work is not done.

Improved writing alone will not make every student a scholar, will not eliminate all high school dropout problems, will not guarantee a successful transition into middle school or into high school by each student, and will not quiet the endless complaints about educational achievement from politicians, community leaders or misleaders, or the media. Educational achievement is impacted by far too many variables for any one action to correct all substandard factors.

Of all the factors impacting educational achievement that educators can control, the factor that matters most is what teachers and students do in the classroom. If the classroom experience is right, education works. If the classroom experience is not right, nothing can compensate. Extreme writing is presented as one source of ideas and activities that can help make classrooms places where abundant, meaningful, real learning is caused.

Keen Babbage
Lexington, Kentucky
July 2009

# ❶

# THE IDEA OF WRITING

**F**or some students, writing assignments and writing projects for school are pure joy, which few other school duties can equal. For other students, writing assignments and writing projects are pure agony, imposing a burden that no other school duty can equal. For still other students, perhaps the largest number, writing assignments and writing projects are merely part of the regular routine requirements that are to be endured without joy and without agony, but with compliance.

This chapter explores the energy, purpose, meaning, and commitment that can emerge from writing that is based on ideas, especially ideas that matter, that inspire, that intrigue, and that are real.

"Just get it finished so you'll have something to turn in. If you don't get your grade up in this class, you can't play in the football game Friday night. If you don't play, we'll probably lose." Jason was irritated at his football-star friend Thomas, who was just not thinking straight.

"Well, if I could write about football it would be worth doing, but who cares about analyzing the main characters in some novel I didn't read?" Thomas was honest about his apathy toward the novel, but that attitude could hurt the football team.

"Nobody cares. Caring is not the point. Turning something in so you can pass the class and play football, that's the point. It's not about writing. It's about football." Jason was blunt.

"Okay. I'll write something about the two main characters. I did not read the book, but the characters probably had some conflict and problems. I'll make up something about that. If I write enough I'll pass, then Friday night I'll catch the game-winning pass. Neat, huh? The word *pass* means almost nothing to me in class, but means everything to me in football. Now that might be worth writing about." Imagine what creative and inspired writing Thomas could do with an essay about a conflict between two football coaches who disagree on what the team's offense should emphasize: *To Pass or Not to Pass—That Is the Question.* That was not the assignment. That was never the assignment.

"Dream on. School writing is not real writing. Just finish this so you make a D grade and are eligible for football." Jason won this debate.

"Okay, Jason, I'll be finished in a few minutes. The paper will be long enough to look serious. I'll make a good enough grade. I just need something to turn in. My grade will be fine. The football team has nothing to worry about."

High school students can benefit from reading and analyzing meaningful novels. Certainly, some high school students are much more interested in the Friday night football game than in the Tuesday morning English class assignment, but could those two events be symbiotic? Is there sometimes conflict on a football team? Is there drama in a football game? Are there some aspects of a novel's story about main characters whose personalities, goals, dreams, and egos collide that are similar to the football-field collisions between players on opposing teams?

What is it about football that motivates a 16-year-old to give his total effort despite possible pain and certain obstacles, when a few hours earlier that same student made much less effort in English class? How could football be played without precise language communication? What is it about football, or any other wholesome high school activity that students dedicate themselves to, that teachers could connect with to make school writing assignments more meaningful, more productive, more real, and more than a task to complete just to have something to turn in for a passing grade?

## FOR TEACHERS ONLY: TEACHING INSIGHT 1

This book is the result of ideas that were expressed through words written on paper. Is that what today's students do when they communicate?

# **1**

It is likely that for most students, the process of communication relies primarily on three methods: talking in person, talking on the phone, or sending messages electronically. Those three options are opposite from the standard classroom writing task, which probably includes a topic provided by the teacher, a pen or pencil, and a sheet of paper.

Students whose most common form of "writing" is a "What r u doin" text message bring an electronic divide with them to the classroom. Formal classroom writing is an essential part of a proper education, despite electronic gadgets and the abbreviations or shortcuts that electronic messages inherently include.

Telegrams used abbreviations and limited wording. Magnificent writing continued throughout the telegraph era and endured after the telegraph era. Computer or cell phone electronic communication may last longer than telegraph use did, but there is still a need to learn formal, structured, linguistically correct academic writing with precise punctuation and accurate spelling.

The most sophisticated thinking cannot be expressed via the least sophisticated writing. The staccato efficiency of telegrams or of text messages serves a purpose; however, ideas that include some depth, breadth, height, and overall substance do not fit into a rationed, minute number of keystrokes.

When students complain that they never write anything beyond a quick computer text message, let them know that the creative, scholarly, academic, substantial, challenging writing you have planned for them is much more intellectual than the vaporous electronic messages they commonly use. You give their brains more credit than a text-message screen can give them.

## THE IDEA OF WRITING: WRITING IS ABOUT IDEAS

The first step in writing is thinking. The first step in creative writing is creative thinking. The first step in real writing is real thinking. The first step in extreme writing is extreme thinking.

There are significant differences between writing perceived as a task to be completed and writing perceived as an intellectual, personal, meaningful experience to be embraced, explored, and valued. One difference is the extent to which the writing is about ideas. Consider a classroom where the teacher always has a writing topic for students to work on during the initial minutes of class, while attendance is taken. Students enter the classroom, socialize, sit in their desks, and glance at the front board to read the topic for the daily writing: "Explain which of the four seasons you like best." Responses from students could include the following:

"I like summer because we are not in school."
"I like winter because snow days cancel school."
"I play baseball, so I like spring, when the baseball season starts."
"It's hard to like any of the seasons except summer, because the weather is so bad in the other seasons."
"I like autumn, which is what my parents call *fall*. It's the season when the temperature is not too hot and is not yet cold, plus our school usually has a fall break in October, so I like that."

The writing prompt required an explanation, but the replies were simplistic, limited, get-it-over-with, who really cares statements. What could be done differently to energize this writing activity with the power of ideas? First, what is the purpose of the writing activity? Is it to occupy students while the teacher checks attendance? Is it to begin today's instruction with initial thinking about one of the topics to be studied today? Is it to improve writing and thinking skills? Is it to comply with a requirement that every class in the school and/or in the school district will begin with a writing task? The writing done by students will probably be of a quality that matches the importance of, the meaning of, the purpose of, the idea of the writing activity.

Second, what will be done with the writing that students complete on the topic of seasons? Is it put away until the weekly or monthly check to confirm that some effort was made on each daily writing activity? Is it read and responded to by the teacher with sufficient frequency and individualization that the students and the teacher truly communicate via writing? If it is for a grade, that often communicates to students that it is important versus a lofty hope that writing could be done for the purity of the experience or that this is just a task not worth the time grading requires.

If a teacher needs students to think about the four seasons and to write those thoughts, how could the writing activity inspire more creativity, more effort, more thought by emphasizing an idea to be contemplated instead of a chore to be completed? "Select the season that you like the most and give it a new name that more accurately communicates what is good and what is unique about this season. Explain two reasons why this name is better than the current name of winter, spring, summer, or fall."

To give a season a new name and to explain the superiority of that new name form different thoughts than to merely state what season is liked best and why. Naming a season takes a student into some analysis of the unique characteristics of a season and takes a student into the intellectual endeavor of precisely selecting the right word to convey the precise idea. The student identifies what is to be communicated, selects the word that implements that communication, and then offers reasons for his word choice versus others. In this process, words interact with ideas, which results in new thinking that expands skills of analysis and writing. How might students respond to the writing assignment of naming a season?

"My favorite season is winter, but the word *winter* really does not tell you very much about December, January, or February. A better name for this season would be *look out*, because the cold temperatures, the snow, the ice, and the driving conditions all mean that you have to constantly look out for anything that could freeze or get snow covered or ice covered. *Look out* is more descriptive and more accurate than *frigidity* or *avalanche*, which were the other names I considered. *Look out* really tells you that this season needs a warning, which means it can be a very brutal season." The idea that people need to look out for the dangers, difficulties, and destruction that winter can bring is a vivid, imaginative idea from which compelling writing can flow.

What is the sum of two plus two? Four. Explain the concept of, the process of, and three applications of addition. Adding two plus two is a finite bit of mental processing. Explaining the concept of, the process of, and the application of addition is an expanded exploratory collection of ideas. When students are told to write about a finite fact, their writing often will have limited style, substance, thought, vocabulary, and meaning. When students are given the opportunity to intellectually explore ideas, their writing can have unlimited style, substance, thought, vocabulary, and meaning.

Of course, finite facts need to be learned in all subjects studied at school. There are some finite, specific, nonnegotiable, creativity-resistant, objective aspects of writing, such as proper verb tense, correct spelling, and proper punctuation. Those facts and objective aspects should not be the plateau upon which education rests; rather, they can be the foundation upon which education builds.

When high school juniors in three U.S. History classes I taught during the 2008–2009 school year were asked individually to tell me the topic in U.S. history they would like to know more about, do research on, write about, and inform the class about, the range of topics they mentioned was fascinating. The list is below. Please read it with the intention of noticing more than the topics; rather, notice what the vast range of topics reveals about these young scholars.

## U.S. History Topics High School Juniors Selected to Research

1. Historical authors
2. Artifacts and photographs
3. The Industrial Revolution
4. The Gulf War of 1991
5. World War II
6. Battles of the Civil War
7. American writers
8. Famous biracial Americans
9. Conservation and wilderness areas
10. How raising the minimum wage impacts the economy
11. The Holocaust
12. How changes in industry affect the environment
13. Medical developments
14. The history of Harvard
15. How religion has influenced politics
16. The 1960s
17. Thomas Jefferson
18. Huey Long
19. The culture of the 1980s
20. The culture of the 1990s
21. The 1920s

22. The *Hindenburg*
23. John Hunt Morgan
24. Economic changes
25. The Vietnam War
26. Gasoline prices
27. Pop culture changes
28. The Beat Generation of the 1950s
29. Life at home during the World Wars
30. The assassination of President Kennedy
31. NASA
32. Why the economy has cycles of growth then recession
33. Unidentified flying objects
34. Political corruption in the late 1800s
35. The rise, influence, and structure of political parties
36. The impeachment of President Clinton
37. Native Americans of the West
38. The Korean War
39. Wars involving Israel
40. The Central Intelligence Agency

The students were eager to do the research. The students enthusiastically wrote about the topics they selected. The students confidently reported in class what they learned. Their research was guided by the following scoring guide, which they were given so they knew what was required. Notice that the research was designed to explore their interests and to deepen their knowledge on valid topics that were meaningful to them.

1. Name:
2. Topic:
3. Most important fact or idea I knew about this topic before this research:
4. Three questions I wanted answered about this topic:
   a. Question:
      Answer:
   b. Question:
      Answer:
   c. Question:
      Answer:

5. Other interesting information, questions, and answers I found about this topic:
6. Sources used:
   a. Print (2)
   b. Internet (2)
7. Most interesting quote from a print source; include the quote and the source:
8. Most interesting quote from an Internet source; include the quote and the source:

The list of topics was more creative and had a wider range than I could have provided. It was my responsibility to design the requirements for the assignment, to interact individually with students as they did their research, to show students the brilliance that is within books, to direct students to high-quality websites and to Socratically ask questions that helped lead students from what they knew to what they were eager to know.

Their research did not create a list of facts about the topics they researched. Their research did create a set of answers to questions. Within the interaction of question and answer were ideas. "I never knew . . ." Or "I didn't know . . ." were prefaces to many sentences spoken by the students as they presented their research findings in class. They proudly and confidently turned in what they wrote about the topics that their interests led them to research. The assignment was my idea. The topic each student researched was the idea of each student. The research findings were an abundance of ideas. From fascinating ideas can come extreme writing and compelling learning.

## FOR TEACHERS ONLY: TEACHING INSIGHT 2

The quality and depth of research done by the students on the history project surpassed my high expectations. They knew they were learning. They eagerly sought to learn more. They confidently and proudly presented their research findings in class. These presentations created an academic atmosphere that aroused insights, questions, and curiosity. The written reports were composed carefully, meticulously, and accurately.

What explains those results? One answer is the power of choice. Each student researched a topic of personal interest and of academic importance. Another answer is that the project evolved as the students became more fascinated with their research findings. The project became their self-driven quest for knowledge. Many of the students wrote more than was required largely because they learned more than they anticipated.

As lessons are designed, as teaching activities are created, as classroom experiences are shaped, the power of choice can be overlooked due to time limits, the crunch of paperwork, the prescribed form that lesson plans must take, inertia, weariness, or frustration. Those factors are part of the reality of teaching; however, the animosity teachers may feel as the education bureaucracy seeks to squeeze classroom instruction into a controlled mold is similar to the "So what?" response some students may have to assignment after assignment that seems to squeeze otherwise unique students into a generic mold.

In order to inspire and to educe the best work from students, there are times when teachers include student ideas in the development of activities or assignments. The teacher is still in charge, yet the students are more involved from the beginning. The partnership this can establish between teacher and students is uplifting for everyone.


## WRITING IS WORK

"The students seem to expect everything at school to be fun. Even their parents or guardians will say that their child or teenager told them how much fun a class was. Fun. I can't make sentence structure fun. The science teacher cannot make the periodic table fun. The math teacher is supposed to teach geometric proofs, not provide geometric entertainment. I can't just let them always pick their favorite activities and topics. I have to be sure they learn what they are required to learn. Writing is work. When I assign essays or research papers, it is to make them work, not make them entertained."

The purpose of extreme writing is not to make writing fun. Writing is work. Extreme writing is work. The purpose of extreme writing is to make the work of writing so fascinating, so meaningful, so rewarding, so real, so personal that it is worth doing and that it is worth doing well. Why permit writing assignments to be perceived as, treated as, and completed as merely something to be turned in when writing activities can be designed as, presented as, perceived as, treated as, and experienced as a meaningful encounter with, creation of, and expression of ideas that are real, fascinating, and important right now in the life a student is living today?

Attach the power of reality, of fascination, of importance, of what matters right now to the writing students, and the results include better writing, more learning, more rewarding classroom experiences, less resistance, more commitment, and a stronger partnership between students and their teacher, which matches the ideals that inspired many people to become teachers. The students may describe the extreme writing process as fun. The teacher will know that the extreme writing process was intellectual, meaningful, creative, purposeful, productive, and challenging. The students and the teacher will use different descriptions, but they are reaching similar conclusions about the value, educational and personal, of the extreme writing experience.

One reason that quality writing is work can be found in the demanding standard of selecting the precise word to express the exact thought. Ideas are as effective as the words that take the idea from conception to birth. From "I have an idea" to clearly, precisely, effectively communicating that idea through writing requires that, for example, the nonword *stuff* can never be used. "She worked for hours and hours only to decide that the stuff she was working on would never be completed." That sentence does the writer and the reader no good because the essential revelation, what is being worked on, is lost in a nonword that generically fills space while expressing nothing.

"She worked for hours and hours only to decide that the precious and treasured family photographs from three generations would require weeks of meticulous effort to properly organize." Now the reader of the sentence can form a detailed mental picture of a family member fully captivated by a labor of love, treasuring each story that accompanies each photograph, and promising herself that she will honor prior generations with a perfectly organized century of photographic gems. *Stuff* cannot communicate such detail and emotion. Quality writing requires thoughtful, quality word selection as the dictionary in the brain edits carefully to make the selection of each word match perfectly with the idea that word is chosen to fulfill.

The extreme writing teacher can gain unlimited insight by listening to conversations of students. There are wholesome topics on which elementary, middle, or high school students are experts. Apply their expertise—they are discussing it often with a friend, so listen carefully, ask questions, take a sincere interest—to the curriculum and create extreme writing adventures where the lesson objective of the teacher applies the resource of student expertise, interest, talent, and knowledge.

Are students aware of how academically connected their wholesome knowledge, talents, and interests are or could become? Do students notice the detailed mathematical analysis that could be written based on the statistics from an athletic event they are discussing? Do those students realize that they could write about those statistics successfully and enthusiastically with direction and guidance from an extreme writing teacher?

Do students notice the science of sounds associated with different musical instruments in a band or orchestra? What scientific analysis could be written to explain the reasons why a trumpet sounds different from a trombone and why both of those instruments sound different from a French horn?

What would high school students who love sports or music think if their math and science classes connected with topics they are very interested in and are eager to know more about? Could those students become extreme writers as their writing topics and their wholesome knowledge, interests, and talents increasingly connect?

"Come on. Get serious. If students just write about sports or music, they will never do any serious writing. They need to analyze the intricate plot development and character transformations of the great works of literature. What would sports have to do with *Romeo and Juliet?*"

That is a very reasonable question. The extreme writing teacher demands the highest level of thinking and of writing. To get to those lofty levels, the extreme writing teacher applies three of the most potentially productive resources that are in every classroom: the wholesome knowledge, interests, and talents of students.

How could the conflicts, disputes, resentments, and animosities of the opposing families in *Romeo and Juliet* connect with the realities of opposing athletic teams? What precise pieces of music—classical, jazz, instrumental, vocal, popular—match with each scene in *Romeo and Juliet*? Those topics would come with required writing standards, yet the standards would make more sense because they encourage and enhance writing that is cared about, that is meaningful now, that relates to students now, and that is personalized for each student.

Why create a stalemate with students who reject thinking about or writing about *Romeo and Juliet* because that play was written hundreds of years ago? Extreme writing connections could show students how much their wholesome interest, knowledge, talents, wonder, and curiosity connect with issues in, ideas from, and characters in a Shakespeare masterpiece. "But I can't write like Shakespeare," a reluctant student named Tasha might express as frustration, as an excuse, or as basic reality. The extreme writing teacher replies, "Good. A second Shakespeare is not our goal. Think as profoundly as Shakespeare thought. Understand and explore his ideas. Then do some Tasha thinking and writing to apply Shakespeare's writing to your thinking, your life, and your writing."

The purpose is not to endure Shakespeare sufficiently to complete a writing assignment and then move on to the next typical, ordinary, mundane, predictable writing task. The purpose is to cause learning. By connecting what students have already made a commitment to—their wholesome knowledge, talents, and interests—with what students need to learn now and write about now, everyone benefits.

Writing is about ideas. Students have many ideas about the endless topics that intrigue them, fascinate them, have already evoked a commitment from them, and are part of their collection of wholesome knowledge, talents, and interests. When face-to-face with some writing topics and tasks, otherwise idea-filled students can encounter a relentless writer's block. "But who cares about the periodic table? Why do I have to write some explanation of what all those numbers and letters mean?"

Students like pizza. What would a periodic table of pizza look like? The different shapes of pizza, the different toppings for pizza, the various cheeses that can be used, the ways pizza can be sliced, restaurant pizza contrasted with grocery store pizza, plus measurements of weights, calories, and nutrition could result in an academically valid version of a periodic table for pizza. The students design this new periodic table, write an analysis of their design, explain the information that is communicated by the pizza periodic table, and then they make the intellectual connection between the pizza periodic table and the scientific periodic table of elements.

Put a pizza restaurant menu in front of students and assign this writing task: (1) analyze the organization of the information that is communicated on this menu; (2) list three suggestions that would improve the format of and the design of the menu; (3) explain whether this is a good menu for communicating to customers or not.

Later in class or the next day, the same teacher and the same students who thought about, wrote about, and then discussed the pizza menu move on to writing about, discussing, and analyzing one of the following: a map, a laboratory experiment, the plot structure of a novel, a geometric proof, a science fair project, a computer program, a presidential inaugural address, or another topic that teachers need students to master. The analysis of the menu creates many compare-and-contrast writing topics when applied to the other areas of knowledge to master.

## FOR TEACHERS ONLY: TEACHING INSIGHT 3

Student conversations are endless sources of writing ideas for teachers. On any and every Monday morning, as students gather in the hallways, the cafeteria, the gymnasium, the library, or the classrooms, there are energetic conversations about varied topics.

A new movie. A restaurant. An athletic event. Homework completed or not completed. A family visit to see grandparents. A part-time job. An outing to the mall. A rumor. A weather forecast of snow. An upcoming school vacation.

Students unknowingly provide conversation topics that can become extreme writing topics. What better way to identify the wholesome knowledge, talents, and interests of students than to hear comments that reveal some of them?

The students who talk about a perfect game in Major League Baseball give an open-minded and imaginative teacher the idea of what would be perfection in science. The next day the teacher and students in Physics class analyze the scientific and mathematical factors involved in a perfect game in baseball. The teacher and the students then identify what is perfection in a physics experiment and in application of the experiment to everyday life.

Students talk to each other whenever they are given the opportunity to communicate. Hearing what the students say, with proper deference to privacy and good manners yet with an awareness that most students usually appreciate it when adults take a sincere interest in them, is a continuous source of teaching ideas that can provide learning connections as part of extreme writing activities.

Writing begins with thinking. Great writing begins with great thinking. The human brain is designed to make connections. Stubborn, defiant resistance to writing can be lessened when the writing topic and task connect with a student's wholesome knowledge, talents, and interests. Why must school thinking and writing serve only school purposes that exist within the confines of a classroom? School writing can connect with parts of life that occur outside school.

A teacher would like for eighth-grade U.S. History students to put themselves on a 1492 boat with Christopher Columbus and write about the journey across the Atlantic Ocean. The teacher hopes that creativity, analysis, insight, and explanations will combine into superior writing. What could the extreme writing teacher do to enhance this writing project and to productively prepare the students for this project?

Some students may have been involved in Girl Scouts, Boy Scouts, or similar organizations. Their experiences could form a connection with the writing topic. Students who are involved in school extracurricular activities may have club, team, or other experiences that relate to a group of people involved in adventures, challenges, difficulties, discoveries, solving problems, and pursing goals. Those students could find similarities and differences between their experiences and those of Columbus.

Writing is about ideas. The best idea is usually not found in one magical moment of inspired intellectual perfection. The best ideas develop over time and with extended work. Thomas Jefferson edited and revised parts of the Declaration of Independence. Abraham Lincoln edited and revised parts of the Gettysburg Address. Writing is work. Revising what has been written and rewriting what has been written adds more labor to the original work. What can be found in the wholesome knowledge, interests, and talents of students that could build commitment to, perhaps eagerness for—well, at least understanding of—revising and rewriting?

The high school marching band invests hundreds of hours in practice to perfect their program for each marching season. They do not sight-read the music, walk through the formations once, and then advance immediately to a performance or to a competition. Rather, they practice, they consider variations, they find a movement that looked good on paper but does not work on the football field, so changes are made. They edit and revise their program. The best marching bands practice, edit, revise, and practice. The same process applies to the best writing.

When a student who accepts and commits to the edit-and-revise process for his or her high school marching band is shown that great writing emerges from a similar process, commitment to the many hours of work needed to take writing to the award-winning level can be enhanced. "Okay. I get it. I'm still more interested in marching band than in writing about that experiment we did in Physics class, but, yeah, I can see the reason I have to rewrite my paper. If I marched in the band the same way I wrote that paper, the band director would not accept my effort. Okay, I'll rewrite this. I'd rather not, but at least I understand why I have to do this."

A marching band's performance is not a random or disconnected collection of notes and steps. The performance is a precisely designed and choreographed sequence of steps matched to be in perfect synchronicity with the notes. The performance began with an idea.

"We want the audience to enter into the dynamic wonder of Broadway's best musicals. Our goal is to inspire the audience so they want to see these Broadway shows performed onstage, memorize all of the lyrics to all of the songs, and brighten their most dreary day with the memory of uplifting music that was performed with energy and inspiration." The idea for that performance began with an intellectual concept that was given force, structure, form, energy, and substance as the program was written to merge music and marching into an idea realized, experienced, displayed, seen, and heard.

Athletic teams, debate teams, quick-recall academic teams, the cast of a school play, the school newspaper staff, the school yearbook staff, the school television or public address system announcement crew, and other school groups are accustomed to editing and revisions. Game plans have to be modified as unexpected game circumstances develop. The staging and blocking of a scene in a school play have to be revised to apply the unique skills of the current cast. The yearbook format for the section about clubs and community service needs to be revised based on awards won by several school groups.

Students accept and experience rewriting and revision in many school activities. The extreme writing teacher can apply this acceptance and experience in the classroom. "What works with your marching band also works with your U.S. History paper that needs to be rewritten."

Logical acceptance may not include perfectly polite, pleasant participation. When I explained a homework requirement to a high school junior my final words were, "Does that make sense?" His reply will forever fascinate me. "It makes sense, but I don't understand." He could logically process and logically accept the reality of what I told him had to be done. He still did not understand why he had to do it.

One step at a time is a legitimate way to measure progress. For that student, the assigned work went from not making sense to making sense, which meant it went from not being done to being completed on time, done correctly, and done well. He completed the assignment successfully but still without a personal benefit he could see other than a good grade. A few weeks later he asked me if I had read a book about an Army special operations group. Within a few days I had read the book and found it absolutely compelling.

The student asked a question in class soon after that. In my answer I included a reference to the book he had recommended. "You read that. You've already read that book." When he later included a reference to the book in an answer to an essay question, a new example of the power of extreme writing had been found. This time, it made sense to him and he understood because it personally related to him and to his life.

Writing is about ideas. Students have ideas. Students have thoughts, opinions, preferences, reactions, habits, inclinations, and goals that relate to ideas. There is a body of knowledge that students must master to gain a high school diploma. The established curriculum of a school,

school district, or state may include specific writing skills or may include other academic objectives that can be gained through a variety of instructional methods including writing.

Each student brings with him or her to school a personal life curriculum that has already been encountered, experienced, explored, learned about, struggled with, and entered in the memory for access and application whenever needed. Students are experts on themselves. They may have as many questions as answers, they may have as many obstacles as achievements, yet their knowledge of, curiosity about, dedication to, and concern about themselves are often relentless.

When the school's curriculum and the student's personal life curriculum can team up, the results are superior. Writing is an essential part of the school's official curriculum. Some students give school writing their best effort; other students do average, barely passing, dismal, or failing work on school writing. Extreme writing seeks to build upon the inherent intrigue students already have with some ideas and the strong commitment students have to their wholesome knowledge, talents, and interests to enhance school writing experiences. These enhanced experiences can be more meaningful for students while also increasing student achievement and thereby increasing teacher job satisfaction.

Is this easy to do? No. Is this the result of quickly and easily making copies of prefabricated worksheets that generically apply to every student in the nation, thus personally or individually applying to no student? Of course not.

Is this the result of an insightful teacher who knows his or her students well enough to connect the wholesome knowledge, interests, and talents of students with the academic content that must be learned? Yes. Is this the result of challenging students while also enthusiastically learning with, from, and about students? Yes. Is this the type of classroom experience and interpersonal experience that inspires the best work from students while creating the most rewarding work experiences for teachers? Yes!

When a school purchases a set of textbooks, the price often includes an abundance of "free" supplementary materials. Those materials include questions, tests, quizzes, reviews, summaries, study guides, enrichment reading, and many technology supplies. The people who conscientiously and professionally prepare the supplemental materials are well informed about the subject matter and are well informed about designing supplemental material; however, those people do not know your students. The writing tasks included in the standard supplemental materials are functional, legitimate, ordinary, and impersonal. Students will not do the best possible writing in response to tasks that are ordinary, impersonal, generic busywork.

## FOR TEACHERS ONLY: TEACHING INSIGHT 4

Worksheets do not work. The prefabricated, ordinary, generic, impersonal worksheets that accompany textbooks may fill the minutes of a class, but they do not fill the minds of the students in the class.

"Imagine that you were a journalist who interviewed Christopher Columbus when his ships landed in October 1492. What questions will you ask him, and what are his answers?" That generic question could be used with any person and any event in history, but it will never inspire the best thinking, work, learning, or writing.

"Some crew members sailing with Columbus wanted to turn back and return to Europe. Instead, the journey continued and the persistence led to success. Think of a time in your life when persistence led to success. Explain how you were able to persist. Identify a similarity in what you did and in what Columbus with his crew did."

Now, teachers, what differences do you notice in those two questions, and what difference would you expect in the finished products from students? Think also of the new knowledge you could gain about your students as you read of their experiences with persistence. Think of additional connections you could make with your curriculum and this new knowledge you gain about your students. Think of the classroom discussion that includes what your students now realize they have in common with Christopher Columbus.

---

The writing experiences students have in the extreme writing approach are uniquely designed by teachers who know their students, know their subjects, know the value of investing time in designing meaningful writing projects, and know the benefits of investing more time in thoroughly reading the writing of each student and then individually responding to the writing of each student. Extreme writing takes thinking, time, and effort on the part of teachers and students. The extreme writing results can be of such high quality that remedial instruction is minimal or is eliminated, thus creating an efficiency in reducing or avoiding reteaching.

The extent to which the extreme writing activities connect what needs to be learned via writing or about writing and the wholesome knowledge, interests, and talents of students is a significant factor in how effective the extreme writing approach will be. Most students like pizza, so the periodic table for pizza could work with most or with many students; yet students in the band, students on a sports team, students who work on a farm, students who are interested in the stock market could write equally instructional papers analyzing the periodic tables they create for band instruments, football plays and positions, farm equipment, or categories of stock market investments.

The prefabricated generic instructional materials are designed to apply to the largest number of teachers, students, classrooms, and schools. Those materials keep copy machines busy, keep students occupied, keep teachers on schedule with curriculum completion dates, and keep thinking to a very basic, limited level. Extreme writing is the opposite.

Extreme writing is designed to provoke thinking, which ignites and inspires writing, which causes learning. Extreme writing helps provide students with the vibrant, fascinating, real, matters-to-me-right-now experience that is the type of life activity students naturally prefer. Extreme writing also helps provide teachers with the vibrant, productive, rewarding student-achievement results and teacher-student interaction that were among the original reasons many teachers decided to become educators.

In the next chapter we will explore the apparent paradox that "students love to write; students hate to write." First one more consideration of the power of ideas will conclude this chapter.

The idea of going to the moon transcended, inspired, and gave purpose to the many scientific, mechanical, mathematical, engineering, industrial, political, and construction tasks that were necessary to actually complete the moon journey. The challenges, the setbacks, the difficulties, the tragedies, the successes, the cost, the labor, the work, the moment-to-moment endurance were parts of the implementation of an idea. The nation was not uplifted by the need to build a bigger rocket. The nation was uplifted by the adventurous pursuit of the idea that human beings could travel to the moon and could then return home safely.

Extreme writing begins with an idea. For example, "Your favorite food is chocolate (each student selects his or her favorite; chocolate is one possibility). Due to health concerns with newly discovered potentially harmful ingredients in some processed chocolates, the U.S. government is requiring that all chocolate products be removed from the marketplace until further notice. Write a letter to one of your senators expressing your opinion of this plan and explaining your suggestion for a better plan."

The writing will use words, phrases, punctuation, sentences, paragraphs, and proper spelling. All of those writing mechanics will be part of effectively expressing an idea that matters, that connects with the student's real life, that connects with wholesome knowledge, talents, and interests of students. The work of writing, the process of rewriting, the task of editing are all worth doing because extreme writing began with an idea that matters, that fascinates, and that justifies the labor. Selecting an actual issue of individual concern to each student and writing a senator about it could also be done.

Ideas are powerful sources of inspiration, curiosity, research, questions, and writing. From ideas come reasons to learn, reasons to search, reasons to think, reasons to endure, reasons to work, and reasons to write. It is in writing about personally meaningful, important, relevant ideas that students are energized to do their best writing and to base that best writing on their best thinking.

Personally meaningful, important, relevant writing by elementary, middle, or high school students is about ideas that connect with the wholesome knowledge, talents, and interests of those students. Because that type of writing, extreme writing, is possible, anything less is an unnecessary limitation on what students and teachers can experience. Having identified the content of, the possibility of, the importance of, and the benefits of extreme writing, we consider now the contradiction, the paradox, the puzzle that says "students love to write; students hate to write."

## 2

# STUDENTS LOVE TO WRITE; STUDENTS HATE TO WRITE

At 10:30 in the morning the bell rings to end second-period class at a middle school or at a high school. Moments after the bell sounds, hundreds or thousands of students fill the hallways. The halls are filled with students and the spontaneous conversations that seem to have begun instantly when the 10:30 A.M. bell rang.

What are the students talking about? Some are not talking; rather, they are yelling, shouting, getting noticed, making sure they are seen and heard. Others may not be talking at all because they are determined to move along efficiently to their next class while making a quick stop at the locker. Most of the students do some talking as they travel from second-period class to third-period class. Listening to their hallway chatter can help explain why students love to write, yet students hate to write. We will visit several hallway locations in a high school during 10:30 A.M. to 10:35 A.M. and transcribe the conversations.

| | |
|---|---|
| Thomas: | That test was easy. What did you think? |
| Andy: | I think that test is over. Nothing else about that test matters. I know I passed. That's enough. Now the soccer coach can quit bothering me about my English grade. |
| Thomas: | Do you have a game tonight? |

| Andy: | We have the most important game of the season tonight. We win this one and we get the top seed in the district tournament. Top seed means automatic first-round win. I gotta go. See ya at lunch. |
|---|---|
| Thomas: | Not today. I'll be in the library during lunch. That paper for U.S. History is taking more time than I expected. |
| Amanda: | Did you hear from that college test yet? I know your score went up. There's just no way that your score from last March was right. |
| Kimberly: | Yeah, it improved. I did better when I took it this summer. I thought it would be better than it was, so I signed up to take it again. It's next Saturday morning here at school, so that means not going to the Friday night football game or the dance after the game. Then after the test on Saturday I work at the grocery store from 2:00 until 8:00. So Saturday is full. After church on Sunday I'll need to do homework all day. This is not what I had planned for my senior year. |
| Amanda: | I know. I'm glad to be a senior, but these teachers act like we're already in college. Read this book by Monday. Write this paper by Tuesday. When do we get to go to all of the school activities? My work schedule is awful. There's just no time. |
| Tasha: | Hey, why didn't you call me last night? At least you could text me during class today? What's with you? |
| Shawn: | That's the problem. I tried to text you during first-period class. The teacher saw me using my phone, so he took my phone. Can you believe that? Instead of giving me a warning he just took my phone. |
| Tasha: | I've seen that happen in some of my classes. What's so bad about sending a text message during class? I can listen to the teacher and text at the same time. So what about last night? Why didn't you call me last night? |
| Shawn: | Well, uh, well, you know, I just forgot. I'm sorry. Hey, I'll be late for class if I don't hurry. |
| Leigh: | Shawn, don't let me interrupt, but let's get to class. The teacher said if you were late again she would write a referral. Let's go. So sorry to take Shawn away from you, Tasha. Maybe he can call you later. |

| | |
|---|---|
| Tasha: | He can't call me without that phone he got taken away. Maybe you can help him stay out of trouble in third-period class, Leigh. |
| Zach: | Turn it up, man, I can't hear that song. |
| Chris: | Neither can the assistant principal. You know they said to keep these things off during the school day. Who cares what we listen to between classes? They make this place like a prison. |
| Zach: | Careful, man, there's an assistant principal heading this way. |
| Chris: | Thanks for the warning. |
| Mr. Jefferson: | Good morning, gentlemen. On your way to third-period class, I hope. The music player goes with me. |
| Chris: | What music player? |
| Mr. Jefferson: | You can make this simple or complicated. The hallway surveillance film will confirm what we both know you were doing. You can't do great work in class if you are listening to some wild music between classes. Give me your name and give me the music player. Your parent or guardian can come get it back one month from today. |
| Caroline: | You did study, right? You promised me you would study. You have to get your grade up in Physics. If we're going to be college roommates next year you have to be in college, which means you have to graduate from high school. You need the physics credit. Why is this more important to me than to you? |
| Paula: | It's important to me. I'll pass Physics. Yeah, I studied some, but I had to work last night, and it was hard to study much while I managed the movie theater concession stand. We weren't all that busy, but my boss decided that everything in the concession stand needed to be cleaned. I'm getting sick of that job. They pay minimum wage, never more than that no matter how hard I work. Then so many taxes get taken out of my paycheck. It's barely worth working for the little bit of money that is left over after taxes. |
| Caroline: | Well, you know, just take your time and think. These tests are not that hard. Remember what we discussed in class and you'll be fine. Don't let this test get in the way of our college plans. |

| Jason: | I had to change my schedule. I've got some new class third period. |
|---|---|
| Ellen: | A lot of ninth-graders got schedule changes. I think it's because so many had bad grades on the first report card. |
| Jason: | Hey, did you hear about those guys who skipped school yesterday? How stupid was that? They came to school, ate breakfast, went home, came back for lunch, hid somewhere, and then rode the bus home. The principal saw them get on the bus; he had just been in their last class, and the teacher said she thought they might be skipping because the teacher saw them at lunch. Boy, are they stupid. |

Ms. Brenda Hunter is a high school teacher. She began class one day with this instruction: "Today in third-period U.S. History class you will begin with a short writing assignment. 'Analyze this: What was the biggest mistake the British made during 1763–1776 in dealing with the 13 colonies?' In five minutes, be prepared to read your paper to us. Are there any questions? No, then begin thinking and writing now."

Ms. Hunter's writing topic and task for her high school juniors in U.S. History class is reasonable. The time period, topic, and task fit the curriculum. Ms. Hunter knows that the essay question on the upcoming test will analyze several 1763–1776 events, documents, and actions, so today's class begins with a writing activity that relates directly to the next test. All of this is logical, sequential, and reasonable. Still, something is missing. Think, please, about what is missing from this writing activity. Think, also, of what could be done to enhance this writing activity so it goes from ordinary writing to extreme writing.

You are exactly correct. This writing task includes no connections between the wholesome knowledge, interests, and talents of the U.S. History students and what those students need to learn about the years 1763–1776. Are connections required, mandated, or necessary? No, connections are not required by law, mandated by policy, or necessitated by regulation. Connections are required, mandated, and necessitated by the standard that says the purpose of a school is to cause learning.

One very effective and very efficient way to cause learning is to make connections with what students know, are interested in, are talented in, and are already committed to. The best teachers meet and surpass the requirements found in laws, regulations, and policies. The best teachers establish higher standards for themselves than could be required by laws, regulations, policies, and employers. The best teachers would not ask, "Are connections required?" Those extreme teachers would ask, "How can I make the most out of connections for my students?" as they eagerly seek to understand how to make more connections to cause more learning.

## FOR PRINCIPALS ONLY: ADMINISTRATOR INSIGHT I

A bill is passed by a state legislature and is signed into law by the governor, directing all public schools to place renewed emphasis on writing at every grade level in elementary school, middle school, and high school. The state's department of education writes the detailed regulations that implement this law.

Each school board in the state is required to approve a policy that implements the new law and the new regulations. Each school must then create a plan to implement the law, the regulations, and the policy, so writing gets renewed emphasis in every classroom. Each principal will provide a report annually to the school district, which provides a report to the state department of education, which provides a report to the legislature and the governor.

School administrators, please beware of such bureaucratic processes as the one described above. Writing quality in a school is unlikely to improve when the dominant reality is, "Well, we have to do this. It's the law. Just do enough to keep the school out of trouble."

The law has to be obeyed. How the law is implemented at your school may have some instructional options that teachers can select from so the power of choice can be applied beneficially. How you present the legal requirements to teachers and how involved you are in implementing the law can impact the success or failure of this new effort. Maybe you could teach a writing class or maybe you visit classrooms much more often than usual and participate in the writing instructional activities.

When you implement what the education bureaucracy imposes upon you, what you implement may be very restricted, specific, and regulated. The extent to which you sincerely and enthusiastically lead the implementation at your school in a human way, not in a regimented bureaucratic way, can help minimize resentment and can help maximize benefits.

Just as student conversations can be sources of teaching ideas, teacher conversations and input can help humanize and unbureaucratize parts of education. Listen to teachers. Students are real people living real lives right now—the extreme teaching, learning, and writing concept reminds us. Teachers and school administrators are real people living real lives right now. Be real. Remind the bureaucracy what reality in schools is. Speak up for the people at your school, speak with them, listen to them.

---

What could be applied from daily high-school hallway conversations to the writing topic in the U.S. History class so connections are made with a topic the students have a wholesome interest in and the important academic topic the teacher needs the students to master? Please think of some possibilities and then read the following option. Contrast the possibilities you create and the one that follows against the original writing task about 1763–1776.

"During 1763–1776 many colonists complained about taxation without representation. High school students who have jobs are taxed, but those students under the age of 18 cannot vote. Explain what high school students today could do to protest their current taxation without a vote for representation."

The topic of the original writing task has academic merit and can be productively included in a lesson. That productivity could increase if the topic of the biggest mistake the British made in dealing with the colonies during 1763–1776 follows thinking, writing, and classroom discussion about whether current teenage workers are subjected to a form of taxation without representation.

The extreme writing about taxation without representation connects with the personal knowledge of and interest of teenagers and their money. The paycheck of a 16-year-old matters right now to that 16-year-old. The paycheck is not theory, textbook, or something to read about only for a test. The paycheck matters now, and U.S. History topics that relate to that paycheck will matter more than if those topics exist in the distant world of another century.

For the high school junior who concludes that too many taxes are taken out of his or her paycheck, a bond is established between that student and colonists of 1763–1776 who resented that so much of their money was absorbed by taxes. What did the colonists do to protest and to make changes? What could a high school junior do to protest and to make changes?

With relevant applications of U.S. History explored through the process of extreme writing, the immediate relevance of history is seen more clearly and convincingly. That academic connection can energize the classroom, the learning, the writing, and the shared experiences of students and teachers.

## STUDENTS LOVE TO WRITE

Music. Athletics. Band camp. Friends. A favorite class. Food. Movies. Video games. Amusement parks. Concerts. Homecoming. Dancing. Graduation. Senior year. Clothes. Television. Theater. Summer. Snow days. The school cafeteria. Malls. Ambitions. Hopes. Dreams. Problems. Money. Jobs. Dating. Technology. Scholarships. A favorite teacher. Parents. State tournaments. College applications. A great book. Art. Politics. Holidays. Vacation. Trips.

The topics listed in the paragraph above are among the many subjects that students participate in, are interested in, are impacted by, are knowledgeable about, talk to each other about, write to each other about, and communicate with adults about. Where two or more students gather, there is conversation. When those students cannot converse, perhaps due to distance or due to time and place, they will sometimes write.

Teachers have confiscated social notes written by students for years and years. No doubt, each generation of students convinced itself that it was the inventor of the "hide a sheet of notebook paper under the paper the teacher handed out and make it look like you are taking notes for class when you are actually writing a friend about some topics of interest." Then, when the teacher turns around to write some information on the board, pass the social note to the other student, hoping that delivery is completed before the teacher turns back around. What are these social notes about? A few examples will demonstrate some topics of the notes and will show that students love to write.

1. "This class is so boring. The same thing every day. Write these paragraphs about the thought of the day. Take notes. Read part of the chapter. Turn in a worksheet. This is so boring.

   Are you going to the dance Friday? I'm grounded, but I'm trying to make a deal to baby-sit Saturday with my little brother and little sister if I can go to the dance.

   Did you hear about Jason? He got kicked off the football team. I heard he cheated on a Biology test and the coach said the team rule was the same for everyone. Jason was their best player. I think his parents are getting a lawyer to fight it.

   Write back, but be sure to finish your worksheet first. The worksheet will be so interesting."

2. "What are you doing after school today? I'm going to play video games at John's house. He got some new game system and a huge screen. Maybe you can come. Did you do the math homework? I forgot so I need to copy yours. You can copy mine next time. Did you read that story for English? I just got a summary from a website. Why read some boring stuff if the Internet will do the work for you? Are you trying out for the basketball team next week? I'll never make the team, but I might try out anyway just to be there. Write back if you can stay awake during this class."

3. "Quit writing me notes. Just quit. Last week when you wrote that long stupid note to me in math class and the teacher took it from me, she called my parents and I'll be in trouble forever. You were so dumb writing about stealing stuff from lockers at school. I can't afford another suspension from school after that one. Your note cost us both five days out of school. My grades are awful. Now everyone thinks we're criminals. We returned the stuff we took from the lockers, but we are big losers now. No more notes. No more crimes. It will take me all semester to get my grades back up. It will take longer than that to fix my reputation. I'm tired of being asked if I'm on the school's ten most wanted list."

4. "That party was so much fun. Robert looked at you all night. I mean he just kept looking at you. He must really like you. Did he

call you or talk to you or text you? Do you like him? My mother almost didn't let me go to that party. She heard that parties at Jennifer's house have alcohol. She talked to Jennifer's mother and father. They said that there was not a drop of alcohol in their home and that they hire a rental security officer to supervise cars, their yard, their house, and the people at any party Jennifer has. So I get to go to the party."

5. "This has been the most boring day. Two of my teachers are absent, and they left nothing for us to do. The substitute teachers had to get videos for us to watch. Boring. Another video about global warming. Then another video about elections. We've been watching these same videos since elementary school. Lunch was good. I talked to lots of people about how to get a job. I need the money. How did you get your job at the restaurant? Do you like it? What's it pay? Could I work there? Can you believe that we are watching a video in this class? At least it is not about global warming. I'd rather watch the video version of the novel I did not read, but this video is awful. The novel was probably worse. What did teachers do before videos were invented?"

6. "The high school counselor talked to my English class today. She told us all about high school. My brother is in high school. He says it is nothing like middle school. I'm kind of excited about going to high school next year, but I'm a little bit scared. It's so big. There are 2,000 people there. We'll be the little ninth-graders. I'm just 14 years old, and high school has 18-year-olds. I guess we'll be okay. There are some interesting classes in high school, but my brother said what's best is all the clubs and sports and stuff. He said that we have to get involved. What are you going to join in high school? I think I want to work on the yearbook or the newspaper. I might act in a play. I'll have to make good grades so I can get a college scholarship. I hope high school is fun, but I think it's going to be hard."

Students love to write. For some students, what they love to write are social notes or an electronic version of that via text message or Internet social network. A social note has nouns, verbs, punctuation, a writer's "voice," a point or impression to make, some information or opinion to express, and an idea. In all of the social notes provided above, the student had an idea that was communicated. English teachers would prefer that proper academic writing have more sentence structure, precise word choice, exact punctuation, and strong paragraph formation; however, the social note format and communication style could be a starting point for some students who love to write, but who hate to write for classes at school. Consider these examples.

1. The governor of our state has accepted an invitation to speak at our high school. The governor will visit our Political Science class before he speaks to the entire school. The governor has requested that each student in our class write a note to him expressing your thoughts about what you think is the most important problem facing the state today.

2. Some students at our school are very concerned about the earth, about the environment, about recycling, and about other green issues. Some other students are not at all concerned about these topics. An environmentally active student writes a note to an environmentally apathetic student, who then writes back. Write those notes with each note being at least three paragraphs.

3. A friend of yours says that the only way she can pass the math test on fractions is to cheat. She is going to make a cheat sheet to take to the test. You want to stop that, so you write a note telling her not to cheat and explaining everything she needs to know about fractions.

4. An actor will visit our class next week. He will portray William Shakespeare. As part of our preparation for the visit, that actor has asked that everyone in this class write a note to another person telling what you like and dislike about Shakespeare's plays.

5. This year the school has a new rule about cell phones and any other electronic device: they cannot be turned on, used, or seen from the moment you arrive on campus until the moment the school day ends with dismissal of the last class. Write the note or the text message you would send after school today to a friend expressing your opinion of this new rule and explaining your suggestion for what the rule should be regarding cell phones and other electronic devices at school.

## CASE STUDY I

The current generation of children and teenagers is very electronic. When the students in my political science class were asked, "How many of you read a newspaper daily?" the "yes" reply was from 10 percent of the students. The question, "How many of you are related to an adult who reads the newspaper daily?" got a "yes" reply of 80 percent. The students said that they get their information electronically and that they communicate electronically. The extreme writing approach does not condemn electronics; rather, this approach builds upon and connects with the students' skills with and commitment to electronics and technology.

Imagine a high school political science class of 26 students, all seniors. Those students are given the fifth topic above as a writing assignment in class. The reader and the author will write a short part of the replies on behalf of the students. Then those replies will become the basis for a complete lesson about several topics within political science.

Paula:    Can you believe this new rule? What are they thinking? Why the drastic change? Why the get-tough change? If a few students abuse their cell phones, why does everyone have to suffer? It's just like our school to overreact.

David:    We hold these truths to be self-evident. That all students are created equal. That they are endowed by their creator with certain inalienable rights. That among these are life, liberty, and cell phone happiness. The students are and of right ought to be free to use cell phones.

Steven:    This makes no sense. This is severe. This is tyranny. This is dictatorial. How do we protest this? How do we change this?

Margaret:    Finally. The students who disrupt every class with their cell phone will be dealt with. I'm so tired of class after class having a phone ring or a student refuse to give the phone to the teacher. The students who are addicted to their cell phones just need to grow up and get over it.

Thomas:    My cell phone got me in trouble last year. It rang during a class, and it was taken by the teacher. The school kept it for a week, and then my mother had to come get it. I just used another cell phone our family had. Nothing is going to stop us from using these during school.

Brad:       It's not the new rule that bothers me so much. I can live without a cell phone for a few hours. It's the way that all of a sudden the school goes from doing nothing about phones to making it a major crime. You'd think they would ask parents and students for some ideas instead of just announcing this new law.

Julie:      We can do something about this. In ninth grade we studied about rights that students have even when they are at school. Maybe we should sign a petition or go to a school board meeting. Maybe the newspaper could interview us. We could write letters to the editor of the newspaper. We could start blogs. We could get a "Save the Phones" website.

Robert:     I want to be the first student who gets in trouble with this new rule, and then I'm going to challenge the constitutionality of the rule. I'll claim that the First Amendment right of free speech is being denied. I'll claim that due process of law is being denied. The national TV news will report on this.

Brian:      Why is this such a big deal to everyone? I heard that the school budget is getting cut, and this year we have to pay a fee for each sport we play—$50 or something like that. If we are going to protest anything, we should protest that new athletic fee. I wonder if people in clubs have to pay the same fee.

John:       This new principal is making too many changes. We can't leave the campus at lunch. No more assemblies. No meetings or activities during the school day for students. No late work can be turned in. Now, no cell phones. What is she thinking? What kind of a place does she think this is?

DeMarcus:   I'd rather be calling you or texting you. In fact, I almost did that just to see what would happen to me, but I did not want to get you in trouble. Maybe everyone should just go ahead and use their phones to see what happens? How can they catch all of us if everyone breaks the rule? Even with surveillance cameras, how can they catch us all?

Tasha:      This is so dumb. Climate change is going to destroy the earth. The economy is in awful shape. People everywhere are hungry or homeless or both. Students here complain about a new cell phone rule. Grow up. There are more serious problems than when and where every young couple in love at this school can call each other or text each other to say how much they miss each other since they were last together 20 minutes ago.

Shawn: I told you so. I told you this rule would change. I even wrote that editorial in the school newspaper last year. I told the students they were asking for a crackdown because they insisted on constantly using their phones. Those calls are unnecessary. All people do is call and ask, "Where are you? I'm here. Where are you? Okay, see you there." It's dumb.

Katie: My mother says she got along fine at school without cell phones. Of course years ago people got along fine at school without electric lights. This is not the past. Cell phones are everywhere. Maybe teachers could send us some information about classes on our phones. I would pay more attention to that than to a lecture.

Rachael: I talked to the principal. She said that one concern is lawsuits. So many students put so much junk on their phones that the school could get sued for pictures people have on their phones and show at school. She said teachers were fed up with their classes getting interrupted by cell phone use. I don't like the new rule, but someday I'm going to be a teacher and I sure don't want my students on their phones during the classes I teach.

Andy: If people would relax, this will go away. It's the start of the school year. The teachers and the principal have to get tough at the start. They can't enforce this new rule. After a few weeks they'll give up. They won't change the rule; they'll just change how they try to enforce it. Relax. This will blow over.

Jake: Some students care more about their cell phone than graduating. I bet some students drop out of high school because of this rule. Maybe that will do some good. Some students come here just to play; they cause the problems or start the fights or waste time in classes; they are late to class, they skip class, and they use their phones all the time. Maybe this rule will get rid of those people who have no real reason to be here anyway.

Morgan: In one of my classes last year there was a big fight because of some text message one student sent to another student.

Everyone in the class could have been hurt. I need my cell phone at school, but to be honest I don't have to use it during school. I need it to check on things after school. I can see why a new rule was added, because so many students were using their phones all day, and the school administrators could not get it back under control, so they added this rule. I can live with the rule even if I don't like it.

Now the reader gets to create the writing that the next eight students would do on this extreme writing activity.

Olivia:

Susan:

Shelby:

Jessica:

Nathaniel:

Judy:

Kim:

Bruce:

The short statements from these 26 students are their versions of a note or a text message (typical text code or abbreviations were not used so clarity could be emphasized) that expresses their ideas about a new cell phone policy. Using these statements as a resource and as a unique body of knowledge, how can an extreme writing teacher build upon these thoughts to reach the goals of the day's lesson? Let's check the teacher's lesson plan: (1) students will be able to communicate a point of view supported with convincing reasons; (2) students will demonstrate an understanding of the point of view that is opposite of their own opinion.

Every student had a perspective on the new cell phone rule. The way the rule was made, the way the rule was communicated, how the rule will be implemented and enforced, how students will comply with or defy the rule, the impact cell phones have on classroom instruction, and legal issues related to cell phone communication were all part of the overall list of issues related to this new rule. The extreme writing teacher could have each student read his or her statement aloud. This involves each student and fills the classroom with a range of ideas.

"Okay. You have heard 26 thoughts on the new cell phone rule. You have not heard the principal's ideas, but that is next. Write the letter that the principal would send to each family in this school explaining the new rule, the reasons for the new rule, and the expected results of the rule. I know you are probably not thinking the same thoughts as the principal so far, but do that now. In persuasive writing it is essential to understand the thinking of various points of view, including the thinking that disagrees with you."

The teacher's goal is to develop the persuasive writing skill of each student. A generic topic could have been selected, such as, "Some members of Congress have suggested a national sales tax to replace the income tax. Which option do you prefer? Write a letter to our member of the U.S. House of Representatives to persuade him to support your preference."

The tax topic is valid, but distant. The cell phone topic is valid and is real to high school students right now. Both topics relate to political science issues, processes, procedures, policies, and legality/Constitutional questions. The goal is to develop persuasive writing skills. The methods of developing those skills are not limited; therefore, connections with the wholesome knowledge, talents, and interests and the lesson objective can be made. Those connections build upon commitments students have already made so the academic work is not seen as separate from all other parts of life.

The students will write the principal's letter and will necessarily have to think from the principal's point of view. This can help them think through reasons and methods that could be used to challenge the cell phone policy. The letters could be shared with the principal. Perhaps the extreme writing teacher makes plans to have the principal visit the class to discuss the topic. From the original note students wrote to the letter written from the principal's perspective to a discussion with the principal, these steps could provide a memorable, productive, and meaningful encounter with persuasive writing.

Students love to write. From the early years in elementary school when mastery of letters, words, sentences and paragraphs are sources of pride, to the middle school writing contest that students eagerly entered, students love to write. From the social note passed in class while the teacher's back was turned to the text message about the Friday night football game, students love to write. From job applications to college applications, the writing may be a laborious chore which takes too much time, but students are willing to write.

Students love to get hired by an employer and students love to get accepted by colleges, so even if those writing tasks are not done lovingly, the results can bring a benefit that is loved. Students love to write or students love to get favorable results from their writing, and the extreme writing teacher can build upon either motive.

## FOR PRINCIPALS ONLY: ADMINISTRATOR INSIGHT 2

Ask teachers what they need most to support them in their work. What will the answer be? "Let's have a massive statewide reform of everything in education, and then after we implement it, be sure the state government makes lots of changes in it and eventually abandons it." No, that will not be the answer.

Would the answer be, "Please ask the school board to pass several new policies that are impossible to implement, such as every student in every class will spend at least 10 percent of class time writing"? That will not be the answer.

Would teachers request more administrator walk-throughs? "Please come to my classroom for three minutes and then send me a written summary of what you saw. Be sure to assume that the three-minute glimpse perfectly represents the time I spent preparing the lesson, the full hour of class, and the time I spent grading the papers that students turned in that day." That will not be the answer.

Time. Teachers will ask that school administrators obsessively, stubbornly, and relentlessly protect instructional time. Eliminate the hour-to-hour interruptions of public address systems and students being allowed to miss class for some unnecessary yet approved minimally instructional activity. Oppose the avalanche of bureaucratic trivia: forms to fill out, meetings to attend, pointless training to sit through, interest group presentations to the faculty as community groups of various motives or agendas seek to advance their cause at the expense of teacher time.

For teachers to develop the writing skills of students, much time is needed. School principals and other education administrators will gain appreciation from teachers if the battle lines are drawn so any waste of teacher time is not tolerated.

## STUDENTS HATE TO WRITE

First let's admit that sometimes teachers and school administrators also hate to write. The following discussion could occur in a faculty workroom early one morning as the copy machines are working continuously, the multiple-choice test-grading machine is in use frequently, the printer is busy with materials being sent from multiple computers throughout the school, and the recycle bin is filling with various paper supplies that served their purpose.

| | |
|---|---|
| Ms. Allen: | This graduate school class is one of the best I've taken. Thanks for recommending that professor. The only problem is all those papers. I want to do good work on each paper, but where's the time to write so much? |
| Mr. Berkley: | I remember thinking the same thing. I took three classes with that professor. He's an expert on school administration. We'll both be glad we did the work when we apply for principal jobs and he writes letters of recommendations for us. He told us that he writes about 30 or 40 letters of recommendations per year for his students who apply for school administration jobs. |
| Ms. Kenton: | Speaking of that, I heard there is an associate principal position opening at Jefferson High School. The application process includes a five-page paper you write about why you should be interviewed and hired. My guess is that's done to screen out people. Some people will refuse to write that much, and some people will show in their writing why they should not be interviewed or not be hired. |
| Ms. Allen: | I know this much: when I become a principal, I will not require teachers to turn in written, detailed lesson plans every week like we've had to do this year. A few teachers did no planning, so all teachers had to spend the extra time filling out those holistic education lesson plan forms. The acronym is funny, HELP, but the fact is they take time and accomplish nothing. |

Mr. Berkley:   There might be more where that came from. I hear that for next year we might have to turn in a weekly summary of the work done in each class to show proof that what the lesson plan said would be done actually happened. All anyone has to do is go to my webpage. The calendar tells you what each class is doing. The homework link has details about projects, tests, or reading. The administrators can access the grade input to see the actual assignments that students got grades for. Why would the administrators make us do more lesson-plan busywork when they can access all of the information they need through the computer system?

Ms. Allen:   They say it's what the school district's central office is mandating. The trend is to show accountability and to central office, that means more forms to fill out. More paperwork. Don't the central office people know that what matters is the work teachers and students do in classrooms, not the new forms we fill out about what we are going to do or what we did?

Ms. Kenton:   The truth is that central office and the state department of education are bureaucracies. They don't see students. They don't know students. They see forms. They know people who attend meetings in offices, or who go to conferences. They write reports. We teach students. The jobs are completely different. I'd love to see anyone from central office or from the state government education offices come do my teaching job for a week.

Mr. Berkley:   I once suggested that everyone at central office should be required to substitute teach one day per month. I was told politely that it was impossible. I was told the reason is they don't have time because of all the meetings they must attend and all of the reports they must write and all of the forms they must fill out. I'd say cancel some meetings or reports and forms so you can come see what schools are really doing and are dealing with.

Ms. Allen:   That gives me a great topic for my next graduate-school paper: how to reduce the unnecessary paperwork teachers have to do. Certainly I can find some ideas from schools that have liberated the teachers from unnecessary paperwork.

Ms. Kenton:    Just be sure that our students don't hear about your re-
               search. They might start looking for ideas from schools
               that reduced the writing that students have to do.
Mr. Allen:     That reminds me. My geometry class is writing a paper this
               week about how geometry is essential when you design a
               sports facility. The soccer players in the class are making
               a presentation of their research and writing on Friday.
               They'll take us out to the soccer field and show how the
               field markings can't be done without geometry. They've
               been so excited about this project. I think we can enter
               their paper in a math competition that could earn college
               scholarships for those students.
Mr. Berkley:   Well, the bell rings soon, so it's time to teach. Have a great
               day and keep me informed about any new writing require-
               ments that are going to be added to our already-too-long
               to-do lists.

Meaningful writing activities that serve a personal purpose and connect with an individualized interest are taken seriously and are completed conscientiously. For the teachers in the above story, the lesson
plan requirements did not serve personal purposes, did not connect
with their individualized interest, and were not meaningful. They were
already designing lesson plans that could be summarized on their web-
pages. They saw no need for further writing about their lesson plans.
They interpreted any further lesson-plan writing as a bureaucratic
busywork burden.

Some students interpret some school writing tasks as bureaucratic
busywork burdens. For teachers, the paperwork is a job requirement; it
must be done or the career suffers. For students, if the paperwork is a
grade requirement, it must be done or the grade suffers.

Extreme writing seeks to provide more productive writing experiences for students through meaningful, purposeful, individualized,
connected writing topics and tasks. The goal is high-quality, correctly
spelled, correctly organized, correctly structured, thoughtful writing
that causes learning about writing and about any topic that is explored,
researched, analyzed, and contemplated through writing.

Why do students hate to write? Let's ask the question differently:
what aspect of writing do students hate? The reality is that students love

to write and students hate to write. It's not writing that is automatically loved by or hated by students. Some writing is loved. Some writing is hated.

What are the elements of writing that are hated and that therefore are done with little or no genuine commitment if they are done at all? Of course, students are not in charge of schools, and they will not like every school task they must complete. Yet if writing can be academically valid, instructionally effective, consistent with the curriculum, and related to the knowledge, talents, and/or interest of students, the results can improve for students and for teachers. Let's ask some students.

Angela:     Writing that does not matter to me does not matter. I mean, if it is not about something I care about, then forget it.

Brad:       I can write even if the topic or the assignment is not all that important to me, if the assignment is not, you know, ordinary. Some of the writing we have to do is pointless. Who makes up these dumb topics? So at least make the assignment sort of interesting. If you expect me to give it some thought and effort, then put some thought and effort into what you are asking me to do.

Rebecca:    I really like to write. I write on my own. I keep a diary. I have some stories I've written. School writing is okay. I do it based on what is assigned. Sometimes I wish the assignments were more creative, but, well, it's school. I really don't expect much creativity in math or science.

Carol:      It's always the same stuff. I thought high school would be different. The only difference in writing for high school is that the assignments are longer and there are more of them. At least most high school teachers I have don't start class with those dumb two-minute writing topics just to get us quiet. The topics for those were always so childish when we did them every day in every class in middle school.

Chad:       Okay. I have this teacher in senior English, and he says we do not pass the class unless we write a 15-page research paper that is just like a college paper. He is serious. I tried to transfer out of the class, but it was too late. Then he said we could select any topic that relates to the curriculum as long as our writing is G-rated, legal, and ethical. So I told him my topic was aviation. I want to be a pilot. He loved my topic. He suggested books written about pilots, about war heroes who flew planes, about how planes are designed and manufactured, about the business of airlines, about flight training programs, the Air Force, and how to get a job as a pilot. It's still a pain to have to do all of the work, but at least I care about the topic. I actually interviewed some pilots, and they are helping me get flying lessons. I'm interested enough in flying to do the paper, plus I'd like to get a good grade because I already flunked two tests in that class and you have to pass senior English to graduate from high school.

Luke: I really hate all of the writing assignments at school. All of them. For some reason, every teacher thinks the only way to prove we know anything is to write about it. So in gym class I had to write about why a team should use man-to-man defense instead of zone defense in certain basketball game situations. You don't write about basketball. You play basketball. This is so dumb.

Anne: Most of us do what we're told to do. We get our homework done one way or the other. We study for tests. It's just one more assignment, whether it's math problems or Spanish translation or short-story character analysis or a science lab to write up or a computer project to do. Some classes are more interesting than others, but it's usually more of the same old stuff. I'd rather not have so much homework, and I'd really rather not have so many papers to write, but that's school. There's nothing I can do about it, so I just get the work done, and you know what, there is always more work to do after that.

Beth: It does not happen very often, but every now and then we get a pretty interesting writing project. Most of what we have to write about is what the teachers have to make us write about. I wonder if they hate making us do all of this dumb writing as much as we hate doing the dumb writing. Are teachers really wishing they could be bold and creative, or do they believe this typical stuff they make us do is important? For me, there's writing I care about, like a text message to a friend or an application for a job, and there is writing I have to do for a grade at school. It's just school. It's just a grade. I know how this is done and I usually get A or B grades on my writing. It's easy; it's just not very interesting.

Paul:        I remember back in elementary school. Writing was so dif-
             ficult for me. Not the ideas for stories; I could make up amaz-
             ing stories and tell them out loud. The actual physical work
             of holding the pencil just right and forming the letters just
             right, that was difficult. Finally, when I was seven or eight, I
             started swimming a lot and playing baseball, and I learned to
             play chess. Somehow those activities helped my eye and hand
             coordination. From then on writing was easy to do physically,
             so I just told stories to myself and wrote them down. Middle
             school and high school writing was not so much stories as re-
             search and information, but I could still say stuff out loud to
             think through it and then write down what I said. I still play
             baseball and chess. Maybe a teacher will let me write about
             baseball someday. That would be one great paper.

Baseball. Is there a connection between baseball and U.S. history?
Could Paul research the racial integration of Major League Baseball as
part of a study on civil rights? Is there a connection to physics? Could
Paul write about which laws of physics apply to the game of baseball and
explain how they apply? Could that extreme idea, thinking and writing,
cause learning for Paul? Could Paul write a short story for English class
using baseball as the setting? Could Paul create and write the script of a
radio play-by-play broadcast of an inning of a baseball game in Spanish
to apply and to expand his Spanish knowledge? Could Paul apply math
to an analysis of baseball statistics and write a summary of what statistics
are most associated with his high school team's wins and separately with
their losses?

Yes, an extreme writing project that is academically valid, intellectually challenging, instructionally proper, and consistent with the curriculum can be created for Paul to do in each of his classes. This takes Paul's
love of, knowledge of, interest in, talent in, and commitment to baseball
and connects all of those wholesome realities with school writing. The
results for students and for teachers can be very favorable.

One reason that extreme writing can be so beneficial and so productive for students and for teachers is that it is real writing. Students are
real people living real lives right now. Students are more likely to commit to, think about, learn from, and work on real writing versus what
they see as typical, ordinary, and "finish it so there is something to hand

in" writing. The next chapter will explore the details of and the power of real writing.

## FOR TEACHERS ONLY: TEACHING INSIGHT 5

When experienced teachers who have taught for 15, 20, or 25 years are asked what has changed in education during their career, one answer that could be expected is, "The job is more difficult." What does that mean? Is the job more difficult because of the national divorce rate, meaning more and more students are from families that experienced divorce? Is the job more difficult due to actions taken by politicians who enact laws about education as if that action alone will correct all problems in all schools? Is the job more demanding as demographics of the students change? For those reasons and for other reasons, teaching is more difficult now than ever before. That trend will continue.

What can be done so teachers can cause learning amid increasingly difficult working conditions? Remind yourself and your colleagues of this truth: we know what works. Teachers who get great results can share their ideas and methods with colleagues who are seeking some classroom activity that gets results. That person-to-person trading of reality-based ideas that have worked already is efficient and is encouraging. Each teacher will need to modify any idea to meet the uniqueness of his or her students and their needs, strengths, or goals. The ideas in this book are presented with the certainty that we know what works and with the spirit of trading successful ideas so teacher time, work, and results are enhanced along with student achievement.

# 3

# REAL WRITING

Extreme writing is not designed to be fun. It is designed to be fascinating, challenging, meaningful, personal, individualized, worthwhile, academically valid, consistent with the curriculum, and productive. Students may describe it as fun, but fun is a lovely by-product of work and of learning that are real. One advantage of extreme writing is that it is real writing, real as in it personally matters right now because it relates to students right now, while still being fully related to school, academic work, the curriculum, thinking, and learning. As another bonus, extreme writing requires no new laws, policies, regulations, or taxes.

Words are portrayals of thoughts. Sentences are illustrations of ideas. Paragraphs are pictures of perceptions. What begins in the brain is manifested through words. Words give structure, precision, manifestation, vitality, certainty, and form to ideas. Thoughts are conceived in the brain. Thoughts are born when they are expressed in words.

When words are written, there is an interaction between the part of an idea that is pure concept and the part of the idea that is that concept seeking shape, form, tangibility, and permanence. A person has a thought and a few hours later tries unsuccessfully to remember that idea. "Now what was it I was thinking? How could I have forgotten that?" Written words give permanence to such thinking and create opportunities for endless interaction with the thinking and for improvement of the thinking.

This thinking and writing adventure can be seen by students as a busywork chore that has to be done so a class is passed, can be seen by students as one more of the typical tasks that fill each day at school, or could be seen as having personal value right now. What puts a writing activity in that last category? One answer is the extent to which the writing is real. Extreme writing is real.

What is real writing? Real writing has personal meaning to the writer. Real writing applies to the real life of the writer right now. Real writing applies and connects with the wholesome knowledge, talents, and interests of the writer. Extreme writing is real writing.

This chapter will emphasize the experiences of three students as they each go through a school day or through school days. The writing experiences that the students encounter are designed to see writing from the perspective of some students, to see writing from the perspective of some teachers, while also seeing writing from the extreme writing perspective. As the reader may already expect, the vast range of writing experiences and perspectives about writing will invite a question to which extreme writing will be presented as an answer.

## CASE STUDY 2

Wednesday night at the Montgomery home was Lauren's favorite time of the week. Lauren's mother, Carol, would prepare Lauren's favorite supper of fried chicken, macaroni and cheese, baked apples, and homemade biscuits. Mom insisted on fresh fruit for dessert, but sometimes a little ice cream was added to the fruit.

Wednesday night at supper was the time that Carol and David Montgomery promised would always be 100 percent Lauren's. Her parents spent lots of time with Lauren. They did not attend some social events or some community activities because Lauren would be a fifth-grader only once, and this final year of elementary school was seen by the Montgomery family as a very important time.

What made Wonderful Wednesday, as Lauren called it, so wonderful? Lauren got to select everything that was discussed during supper. Topics ranged from some new clothes she was interested in to her interest in starting to earn money by babysitting. Mrs. Montgomery silently wondered how her baby could be old enough to babysit, but such thoughts just added to the importance of spending much time together now.

Topics had recently included the possibility of attending a sports camp in the summer, the upcoming fund-raising auction at school, the new family that had moved into a nearby home, and the cute fifth-grade son in that family. Mr. Montgomery had hoped it would be many years before his daughter noticed boys or was noticed by boys, but life would go on.

Tonight Lauren's discussion topics were almost all about school. She did mention "the best concert ever that everyone is going to and I really, really want to go to, please." Her parents decided that if she earned the concert-ticket money through babysitting, she could go if one of them or the parent of a friend chaperoned. Lauren was not surprised by either condition. Babysitting and a chaperone were small sacrifices to make for the ultimate concert.

Other than the concert, Lauren's topics on this Wednesday were about school. Her parents listened, answered questions, and gave advice. Lauren's ninth-grade brother, Michael, concentrated on the food more than on Lauren's topics, but he did offer some suggestions as only an older brother could. Lauren's older sister, Michelle, was a freshman in college, so she was home only for holidays or vacations. As the meal was served and the family shared prayerful words of thanks, Lauren began the discussion.

"Well, today in science class we had this big assignment to start working on. It is so much work. The teacher said that next month we will have a science fair and everyone has to have a science project. It sounds like a whole lot of work and stuff, so I might need some help."

Dad asked, "Are other people allowed to help you or are you supposed to do all of it yourself?"

Lauren handed her father the science project instructions, "We got a copy of all this today. It's on the teacher's webpage, so I printed an extra copy. It says you can help me with part of it. There's a long, long paper I have to write about the science project. I have to write it all by myself and I have to type it on the computer. This science project sounds too serious. Science should be fun. This project sounds like it's a punishment or something. Do you know why fifth-graders have to do science projects? I don't think it's fair."

Mom had an answer. "You've visited the hospital where I work. All of the doctors I work with and all of the nurses I supervise base their medical decisions on science. People do research to determine what medicine or what procedure can help people get well. So everyone benefits from scientific learning like you'll be doing."

Lauren was not fully convinced. "But I'm going to grow up and be a television news reporter. I'm not going to be a doctor or a nurse. Why do fifth-graders who are not going to be scientists have to do this project and then write a long paper about it? I still think it is no fair."

Michael agreed. "I know what you mean. Teachers have been assigning more projects every year. It's like they have some contest to see which teacher can give us the most difficult project with the longest paper. It's no better in ninth grade. Sorry, Lauren."

What did Dad think? "Lauren, you could be the television news reporter who is told to do a story about work done at a local hospital. If you are the reporter who knows something about science, you could have an advantage. And that television news story has to be thought out and written. It's to your advantage to know how to think and how to write well. This project could help with both of those."

"What is your project going to be about?" Mom asked.

Lauren smiled as she finished swallowing a bite of the Wonderful Wednesday supper. "Food. I'm interested in food, so I want to create some science project about food. Maybe it could be about healthy food and junk food. Our teacher always tells us to eat the right food, but even at school our lunches don't always have super-nutritious food. I think our teacher complained once and was told that the students won't eat the most healthy food. Maybe that's a good science project. Is school cafeteria food healthy?"

Michael knew all about this. "Just wait for high school. We have a pizza line in the cafeteria. You can get pizza every day. Healthy or not, it does taste good."

Back to Lauren. "What's worse than the science project is that for social studies I have to read a biography of some important American from history. The book has to be at least 150 pages long—150 pages! We have one month to do this, but there is a report due in two weeks on the first half of the book and then another report due in a month on the second half. Two reports. If the book has already been written, why should I have to write anything about the book? I'm not the author. I'm just the reader. How does it make sense for a fifth-grader to write about what some adult wrote in a book? You know, school just keeps getting harder and harder."

Michael was impressed. "Lauren, that's the smartest question you ever asked. There's no real reason you have to write a paper about a book except that's what schools make us do. It's always like that. You are ready to finish elementary school and move up to middle school." Lauren smiled at the unexpected praise from Michael. Mom had a different perspective.

"I can see your point. The author is the expert on the topic, so the author wrote the book. The teacher wants to know your thoughts about the book. You are the expert on what you think about the book. Maybe you could think of the paper you write on the book as a television news reporter who interviews a famous author who visits our city."

Lauren had not thought of that. "Good idea, Mom. If everything at school could be done like a television news program, it would be a lot more interesting to me."

Dad had a question. "I'm always interested in what you are doing in math class. The accounting work I do uses math all the time. So what did you do in math today?"

Lauren knew that her father loved math. She is good at math but is just not very interested in it. "You know, problems and more problems. Mostly word problems. The teacher said it was beginning algebra and stuff. The work was easy. It's just fancy adding and subtracting, the teacher said, with some fancy multiplication and division. There was one part I did not like at all. We have to write a one-page paper explaining what we thought algebra was and explaining how we would describe algebra to a fourth-grader. To be honest, I think the fourth-grade teacher should explain algebra to the fourth-graders, but you know, I won't say that in my paper. It's due tomorrow, and I almost finished it in class. Want to hear what I wrote?"

Everyone smiled. This was Lauren's center-stage night at supper, so she read her paper.

"It's just numbers. There is nothing unusual about numbers. Your address and phone number, those are numbers. Your birthday has numbers.

Math is just numbers. The difference with numbers at school and numbers in real life is that school numbers are just for school. Real-life numbers are for concert tickets or the price of neat new clothes."

"Algebra is no big deal. It's just more numbers, except when a letter is used to take the place of a number. That does look weird at first, but the letter eventually becomes a number. It's not magic. It's just math."

"So in algebra, it's like the teacher tells you that four students eat a pizza that had eight slices. Each student ate the same number of slices of pizza. How much pizza did each student eat? Easy, isn't it? You can figure it out in your head, but the teacher makes you do an equation like $4x = 8$. I'd suggest an equation of 4 people = 8 slices of pizza, but it's not done that way. Too bad."

Everyone was impressed, Mom especially. "Very good thinking, Lauren. You've got algebra figured out."

"Yeah, I know, it just seems so, you know, dumb to have to write a paper about math. Math is numbers. English class is words." Lauren was speaking for many students without realizing it.

Dad had an idea. "Hey, Lauren, I heard you mention that your best friend's birthday is soon. You and Katie are still best friends, right?"

Lauren nodded as she gave the ice cream more attention than the fruit that the ice cream covered.

"Well, would a concert ticket be a good birthday present for you to give Katie?"

"Yeah, Dad, it would be the best birthday present Katie ever got, but how do I buy her a 42-dollar ticket?"

"Well, Lauren, you do two things. You babysit enough to earn 42 dollars for your own ticket. Then your mother and I will match that 42 dollars if you write a paper explaining why a concert ticket is worth 42 dollars."

Michael spoke up. "You never did that for me when I was in the fifth grade."

Mom laughed. "Okay. That's true. You earn 42 dollars babysitting or cutting grass or something else and we'll make a deal with you."

Lauren loved the idea. "Great idea, Dad. Thank you. Thank you. I'll make the money first. Katie will be so excited. Maybe I can use the paper I write for you someday in math class. Finally a paper about something real that I really care about and that really matters. If my teachers did this, I'd be a great writer. Well, I need to call people and find babysitting work. Supper was great. Thanks for having my favorites. I don't have to write a paper about supper, do I?"

Mom answered. "A thank-you note would be nice."

Lauren went along but had a better idea. "Mom, how about a thank-you hug?" Mom agreed that Lauren's idea was perfect.

## CASE STUDY 3

And then there are the middle school years. These are the years when parents and guardians ask teachers, "What happened to my child? She was so cooperative and level-headed. She was so eager to please and so caring. Now no two days are alike. She cooperates on Monday and is defiant on Tuesday. She is sensible on Wednesday and makes no sense on Thursday. Where did my sweet child go?"

Your child may be wondering about the same changes, only using different words. "I'm not a child anymore. Don't treat me like a little girl." can be followed by, "Mommy, Daddy, everyone is being so mean to me. Even my best friends are so mean. They aren't my friends now. Why are people being like that? Can you make it better?"

Middle school teachers can be seen in two groups: those who apply the curiosity, energy, spontaneity, unpredictability, and blunt directness of middle school students to the learning process and those who seek to get middle school students to sit down, be quiet, be still, complete worksheets, and pay no attention to anyone except the teacher for three years. In this case study both of those middle school approaches will be observed.

Luke Morgan was "so ready," as he expressed it, for eighth grade. His sixth- and seventh-grade teachers had worked very effectively with Luke to get his reading skills up to and then beyond grade level. Luke went from "I hate to read" to "When do we get to read?" because now he could read as well as anyone in middle school was expected to read. He actually liked getting to school early and going to the library to see what new books were available.

The first week of eighth grade was not quite what Luke expected. He was told by his first-period teacher that the teaching team Luke was on had four teachers and 110 students, but that the students would not have every teacher every day. This team would have elective classes first and fifth periods. Luke liked art, computer, physical education, and drama electives. He hoped to have all of those. Second through fourth periods would be a big block of time with one teacher. Sixth through eighth periods would be another long block of time with another teacher. So Luke would be with his four main teachers for a block of time every other day. That was not the only change.

After one week Luke had almost memorized the words he had heard from all of his teachers in math, social studies, science, and language arts classes. "Your eighth-grade year will emphasize writing. That is why the schedule is organized in blocks of time. Each block will include a variety of activities, but will always include writing. The types of writing will vary, but be ready to write, write, and write."

Luke's best friend, Brad, was on the other eighth-grade team. That team did not use the block schedule plan. That team had decided that math and science fit together well, so everything done in those two classes was closely coordinated to fit logically. A science experiment would match up with math problems that related to the science experiment so on the same day math and science were two parts of the same topic. The social studies and language arts teachers had similar plans, since their classes were closely connected. The teaching team had arranged the time so the morning class periods included two main classes and one reading period while the afternoon class periods included two main classes and one study-skills period.

During the second week of school, Luke began to wonder if this eighth-grade year was going to work out or not. He and Brad talked about it one day at lunch.

Luke:    I hate it. All morning after computer class I'm with the same teacher doing the same stuff. Then after drama class I'm with the other teacher doing the same stuff. Almost all we do is write, and it's dumb writing. The teachers have these huge books they read from and then we write about whatever they read to us. The teachers are just following a script. I hate it.

Brad:    You'd like my teachers better. We write a lot, but it's always something interesting. We did a science experiment about how bubble gum is made. We did all kinds of math problems about the prices of different brands of gum. We researched the history of gum. We even used gum commercials in language arts class. I never expected gum to be the topic at school.

Luke:       That sounds better than my topics. The worst was in science yesterday. We had to imagine that we were a tree, and we were supposed to explain the process going on that was different in each season during the year. I probably got a bad grade because I wrote that the people who own the land where the tree I wrote about had been growing decided to cut down the tree so they would have firewood. My father and I cut a tree once for that reason. So I wrote what I knew was real. The other stuff we write about is worse than tree stories. This year is really awful.

Brad:       High school will be better. We can pick our classes. There are more sports and clubs and, you know, more girls and dances and stuff. All we have to do is get to high school, and then things will get better.

Luke:       I hope so. Are you sure that in high school I won't have to write anything about being a tree?

Brad:       No way. High school is real. The classes are better. Middle school teachers baby us all the time.

Luke:       Are you going to football practice today? You missed it yesterday. Finally we got to put on all the equipment and then we started hitting and stuff. It was so cool. I'm a little sore, but I can't wait to get there today. Why can't classes be more like football?

Brad:       You mean blocking and tackling in the classroom? That would get you in trouble.

Luke:       No, I mean doing something I care about. If they just let me read about football and write about football, that would be great. But no, I have to write about being a tree. Why can't I write about being a football player, since I am a football player?

Brad:       Because it's school. There are classes and then there's football. Classes are, well, you know, just classes. Football is cool. Football is real. School is just school.

Luke:       There's the bell. I have to go become a tree or a fish or who knows what. I wish I could just be me.

Brad:       You can at football. Hang in there until we get to do some real blocking and tackling today.

Middle school schedules can be arranged in various ways. Students could have eight class periods per day, six class periods per day, or the school day could be divided into blocks of time. Teaching teams could divide the daily schedule so classes meet each day, every other day, or with some hybrid plan. The schedule is not the most important variable. The vital variables are what is taught and how that curriculum is taught. The goal is to cause learning, not to follow fads or experiment with trends.

Students are real people living real lives right now. When school connects to the real lives of students, the results are enhanced with more meaningful results for students through learning experiences that inspire commitment.

These learning experiences that create better results for students also are more rewarding for teachers. There is no bureaucratic solution that creates the perfect reform of education. Making the most productive, meaningful, fascinating, personally relevant, and individually connected learning experiences in classrooms can do more to improve student achievement and teacher career satisfaction than all bureaucratic reorganizations or legislative reforms of education combined. Case study 3 is an example of what can be done, but first some insight for principals.

## FOR PRINCIPALS ONLY: ADMINISTRATOR INSIGHT 3

An idea presented by a group of educators at a national conference about what worked at their school with, for example, a revised middle school curriculum and class schedule is very different from what is created by and for the people at your school.

Ideas presented at national or state conferences are genuine. The people making the presentations provide accurate information from their experience or from their research. No presentation at any national, state, regional, or local conference for educators is designed to convince people that the topic of the presentation is a dismal failure that must be avoided. Presentations tell the wonders of an innovation, a testing system, a revised curriculum, a trendy social engineering objective put into a grant proposal that got lots of funding support, or tell of similar sensational school stories.

Beware. "Well, at the national conference we were told that the new trend is to eliminate grade levels in middle school. The students are not sixth-, seventh-, or eight-graders anymore. They are grouped in each sub-ject based on placement tests. They finish middle school when they show mastery of the total curriculum. It may take some students two years to complete, but three years is most common and four years is a possibility. Every student leaves middle school ready for high school. We'll probably change to this next year." Resist the urge to impose all of the apparently good ideas you hear about at a conference, workshop, or meeting.

Each school is unique. You know your school. The teachers of your school know the students at the school. Consider many ideas that ad-dress the unique needs of and goals for your school. Do not duplicate what the school in another state did merely because it sounds good and because you are getting bureaucratic pressure to do something. Do not reject ideas from other schools merely because the idea was not invented at your school.

Think. Listen. Work with colleagues. Seek input. Build consensus. Emphasize results, not whose idea "wins." Lead. Be the principal you promised yourself you would be when, a few years ago as a teacher, you told yourself you would be different from the principals you had known who imposed the annual school reform plan only to replace it one year later with the new annual school reform plan.

## CASE STUDY 4

"You won't believe what we did in Physics class today. It was so cool. The teacher asked us on Monday what our favorite method of transportation was. The answers were all over the place. Planes. Cars. Subways. Walking. Bicycles. Skateboarding. Then on Tuesday we did all kinds of research on the history of those transportation methods. Today was the best. We compared the cost per mile for each system to carry one person. We used force and mass and all the equations, but we also talked about pollution and green energy. Since I'm the ultimate skateboarder, I did that topic. I never thought Physics would be all about my favorite way to spend time."

Brian's excitement about Physics was a surprise to his girlfriend, Claire. "Brian, you never like school. You never get excited about any class. Are you sure you actually went to Physics class? You didn't skip school and go to the skateboard park, did you?"

Brian pretended to be astonished. "Me? Skip school? You must be kidding. Okay, so I have sort of skipped school before to go on that trip, well, on two or three trips, but if Physics class makes me a better skate-boarder, I'll never miss Physics."

Claire was still concerned. "Oh, great. You'll go to Physics and be the best Physics student. Now how do we get you to attend your seven other classes with the same determination to do great work always?"

Brian knew the answer. "Just make those classes about skateboarding and other neat stuff. I'll be there early, ready and sitting in front. I do good work in school, but in Physics today I did great work. So, what did you do in your Physics class today?"

Claire groaned. "We watched part 3 of some movie about the solar system. Our teacher is out of town at some meeting, so she left these movies for us to watch. Boring. Easy, but so boring. Most people don't pay attention. Two more days of movies. Boring."

It wasn't Brian's choice, but his senior year of high school had to in-clude two science classes. There was some graduation requirement that he had to fulfill, and the science credit he did not earn as a sophomore because he took an extra world language class offered that year in Japa-nese meant he had to take two science classes now. He thought Anatomy class was the best choice after Physics, so his schedule included those two science classes. Brian surprised Claire again. "Oh, yeah. Anatomy class today was really cool. Kind of like Physics was."

"Wait a minute. You did the same cool stuff in Anatomy class that you did in Physics. This is not fair." Claire was right.

"It's like the Physics teacher and the Anatomy teacher worked it out together. Today we analyzed what happens to the human body during different transportation experiences. It was so cool. Astronauts have a tough job. Their bodies take a beating. Pilots of big planes go through some brutal training. Skateboarders break bones, I should know. You know, this physics and anatomy stuff makes me want to be a scientist."

Claire had a question. "Well, is it just fun and games, skateboards, and space travel, or is there some actual work and stuff, you know, like a test or a paper to write?"

Brian sounded proud of himself as he answered. "Oh, there's lots of work to do. Really hard work. It's not fun and games, although, come to think of it, it is pretty much fun. Anyway, yeah, there's work. We write all the time."

"What kind of writing?"

"It's not like the papers we write for English where you describe a character in a play. It's neat writing. It's real. When I get to write about skateboarding, it doesn't feel like work. It's interesting to me, so I get it done."

Claire persisted. "But what kind of writing is it? Essays? Opinions? Persuasive? Research?"

"It's all that. Look, here's the list of assignments I have to complete on this transportation topic just for Physics. Not everyone has the same topic or the same papers, but we all have the same amount of writing. I have three papers to write. First, I have to interview 10 people about their favorite form of transportation. Then I have to find five public opinion surveys about transportation. I analyze all of that data. Second, I have to write a recommendation to the city council and the mayor asking them to build another skateboarding park. Third, I have to create a 30-minute workout plan for people of various skill levels using skateboarding as the exercise method. I can do this as a paper and as a video or just as a paper. I have to show how physics helps make exercise more effective if you use the laws of physics in your favor. Neat, huh? Three very real writing assignments, but I don't mind doing them. It's actually pretty cool. Who ever thought that I would say that anything at school is cool?"

Claire was frustrated. "This is so unfair. I've got this massive science paper to write. I have to analyze the work of one famous physics expert. Do you know of any famous people in physics? Famous people are on television or in movies or in sports. If you are in physics, you are not famous. The paper has to be 10 pages long with all kinds of sources, including books. You sure lucked out."

"I'll probably end up writing 10 pages or more. It's just more interesting stuff. I guess there's not much you can do about your research paper. Just put up with it."

Claire was more and more exasperated. "Yeah, I'll put up with it. I wish I could write about something interesting, you know, something I really care about."

Brian had some hope. "Maybe you can do that in your Political Science class. We're researching political issues. I chose alternative energy, and it's kind of neat because if you use physics to make decisions about energy, you make better decisions. I told my Political Science teacher that the energy problem would be solved by physics more than Congress, and he was really impressed."

Claire could only dream. "Yeah, well in my Political Science class we have to outline chapter 6 and answer all of the questions at the end of the chapter. Big deal. Let's forget all of this school stuff for a few minutes. Any good movies to see this weekend?"

"Yeah. There's a new movie all about skateboarding competitions. Let's go to that."

The purpose of a school is to cause learning. Writing is a specific skill that schools are expected to cause each student to learn. Necessary and desired writing skills go beyond the fundamental, functional basics of constructing sentences and designing paragraphs. The highest-quality writing is correct in mechanics including word choices, capitalization, punctuation, spelling, and structure of sentences or paragraphs; however, the highest-quality writing also has creative, imaginative, compelling, convincing, logical, stylistic, and/or forceful elements that extend the impact of the mechanics.

A great thought poorly written does not appear to the reader as a great thought. A questionable thought written with more quality of writing than quality of thinking will be discovered for its flaws, but will force the reader to be especially discerning. A great thought expressed through superior writing can have vast impact. To teach students how to think critically and to express quality thinking through quality writing is the type of educational achievement that equips a student with skills that are useful for a lifetime. Extreme writing can help make that happen.

What can be done so students master the mechanics of proper, correct writing while also mastering the qualitative aspects of superior writing? What can be done to get this type of writing completed by students at various grade levels and in a variety of subjects? The extreme writing approach is to connect what students need to learn with their existing wholesome knowledge, talents, and interests, yet to do that according to proper writing standards.

Let's think of writing topics, activities, and assignments that students can expect to encounter in school year after year. Please note: students often describe school as boring. If boring means there were no roller coasters, no Hollywood special effects, and no pizza delivered to the class, then boring is accurate. School is not designed to or obligated to amuse, entertain, or cater to snack preferences. School is obligated to and designed to educate, which ideally means to cause learning.

The indictment of boring is common even if the teaching and learning were very effective. Checking for proper spelling may be boring, but it is necessary for high-quality writing. When a student is fascinated by, personally connected with, individually interested in, and sincerely committed to the writing topic and task, there are reasons to do the extra work, including the ordinary work of checking spelling. When the work is meaningful to you, then the quality of the work is important to you. Learning can be caused in fascinating ways, so why not apply the many advantages for students and for teachers that the power of fascination can bring?

Another note: the job of teaching is more demanding, more complex, more analyzed, more measured, and more exhausting than ever. Very few of the critics of schools or of teachers are willing to actually come work in classrooms. The increased demands placed on teachers to make every student fully successful despite some very difficult obstacles or barriers beyond a teacher's control can lead to job frustration. Some teachers then just default to using last year's or last decade's lesson plans or, even worse, to just using the prepackaged, prefabricated materials that came with the textbooks. For teachers and for students, extreme writing can invigorate the teaching and the learning process.

Yes, of course, students should care about doing the best possible writing including profound ideas, precise punctuation, accurate spelling, strong sentences, and powerful paragraphs. Yes, of course, students should complete all assignments conscientiously. Most students do what they are supposed to do most of the time; however, some students do far less than they are required to and other students who meet or surpass all requirements could do higher-quality or higher-quantity work.

Educators have the responsibility to search for, to create, to use teaching methods that maximize the classroom experience for everyone involved, teachers and students. With that thought in mind, let's search for and create some real writing—extreme writing—adventures and contrast those with writing that is not real.

If Lauren's fifth-grade science teacher would like for her students to analyze winter, spring, summer, and fall, there are many possible writing assignments. Some are listed below, and there is space for the reader to include more writing assignments.

1. Compile a fact sheet about each of the four seasons. Include 10 significant facts, such as duration of the season, typical weather patterns of each season, seasonal economic variations such as products people buy in one season but do not buy in the other three seasons, or how the seasons differ across different parts of the United States and different parts of the world.

2. Create a modern legend, myth, or parable that explains how the four seasons began. Tell how your story is similar to and different from scientific explanations for why there are four seasons.

3. Write a one-minute radio or television commercial for each season. Your goal is to convince listeners or viewers to call in and vote for the season they like best so each season, through its commercial, is competing for votes.

4. Use five different dictionaries to get five different definitions for each season. Then write your own definition for each season.

5. Imagine a new board game called The Four Seasons. Create the deck of 52 cards used to play this game. There are 13 cards about each season—write the information that goes on each card. Explain how the game is played—the game and the playing of the game relate completely to the seasons.

6. Complete the four worksheet packets you were given. There is one packet for each season. Pages 47 through 68 in your book will help you complete this.

7. Imagine a new superhero group of comic book characters called The Four Seasons. Describe each of the four characters, giving details that show how the personality and the powers of each superhero relate to his or her season name—winter, spring, summer, and fall.

8. Write a one-page report about each of the four seasons. Include facts, descriptions, and unique characteristics of each season.

The goal is to cause learning about the seasons. A writing activity is going to be one part of the learning process, although more than one writing activity could be used. Put yourself in the role of the teacher whose duty is to cause learning and evaluate the eight options presented above. Then put yourself in the role of the student who hopes that the learning process will include something interesting. Which of the eight activities would most effectively reach the goals of the teacher and of the student?

Now, with the insights and the knowledge you have about your students, create the most productive writing activity that will cause the intended learning while also connecting the seasons with the wholesome knowledge, talents, and interests of your students. Yes, you may decide to create several activities so students can select the one with the most appeal to them. There is power in choice. There is commitment building within choice. The combination of extreme writing and choices can multiply the student achievement results.

In the middle school case study the students wished that the academic experiences at school could be more like their football experiences at school. The students cannot be allowed to play football all day, but academic work could connect all day with football or other activities that motivate students. For example, the statistics associated with athletics measure every specific aspect of each sport for individual athletes and for teams. Many of the specific math skills in the middle school curriculum can be taught through sports statistics calculations and analysis instead of resorting to the generic "two trains left a station" word problem that does not relate directly or at all to the lives of some, perhaps many, students.

Please reflect on the chart in table 3.1 and then complete it. Your goal is to create at least one extreme writing activity that relates to the real lives that students are living right now for each middle school subject listed in table 3.1.

Now the reader will do some real writing. First, please read case study 4 again to get better acquainted with Brian and Claire. Think of two high school students you know. Write the conversation those students could have about school—what they like, what they dislike, what classes they take very seriously, what classes they make less or little effort toward, what they are concerned about, what they hope for, and

**Table 3.1**

| -1- | -2- | -3- |
| --- | --- | --- |
| Middle School Subject | Wholesome Knowledge, Interest, or Talent of Middle School Students | Extreme Writing Activity That Connects 1 and 2 |
| Math | Athletics | |
| Science | Movies and television | |
| Language arts | Money | |
| Social studies | Amusement parks | |
| Art | Board games or video games | |
| Drama | Commercials | |
| Health | Food | |
| Physical education | Summer vacation | |
| Band, chorus, orchestra | Popular music | |
| Computers | Cars | |
| World languages | Dancing | |
| Character education/obeying rules | Making friends | |

other real topics that your two students will have a wholesome discussion about.

When you complete the script, think about what the high school curriculum includes and then create some extreme writing activities that will be academically valid and that will be real writing. The "realness" of the writing will be its connection with the wholesome knowledge, talents, and interests of the students plus its acknowledgment of the fact that students are real people living real lives right now.

Also think about the scoring guide(s) students would be given with the extreme writing activities you create. The scoring guide will inform students about how their work will be graded both in terms of content and in terms of writing mechanics. Ideas count. Spelling counts. Good ideas expressed through correctly spelled words are taken more seriously and have greater impact than great, good, average, or below average ideas expressed in faulty writing.

In the next chapter the emphasis will be on analyzing and creating many extreme writing activity examples. Another emphasis in the next chapter will be getting in the habit of using the extreme writing way of thinking and of writing as a classroom community is built.

## FOR TEACHERS ONLY: TEACHING INSIGHT 6

For some students, the process of writing is similar to the requirement to eat vegetables before earning dessert. A student endures the writing to get the grade that avoids a punishment or a failure. Avoiding punishment and avoiding failure are not lofty goals and are not inspirational experiences.

Students come to your class with opinions of school, with perceptions of teachers, with work habits, or with a lack of work habits. Teachers hope that the school year begins with an eagerness, with a commitment, with a renewed dedication by everyone in the school that this will be the best school year ever.

There will be problems, frustrations, and disappointments. There will be achievements, joys, and progress. There is no one school day that defines or controls the entire school year. It is never too early or too late to create an extreme classroom where extreme writing is part of the extreme teaching. That causes extreme learning.

# ACADEMICALLY VALID SCHOOL WRITING THAT FASCINATES STUDENTS

"**O**kay. I get it. Even the best students may sometimes just go through the motions to complete assignments and make an A. Some of them care about the A, not about the learning. Others are really excited about school and make an A because they care about learning. Then still other students are comfortable with an easy C or an easier D, just enough to pass. For students who refuse to do any work, I can't make the writing real enough to wake them up long enough to write a sentence. Don't the students have some responsibility to do what teachers tell them to do? Don't the students have to do the work, even if it is not their favorite class, because that's their job? Some schoolwork is just a matter of pounding information into your brain. It's no fun, but it was not intended to be fun. It is work."

A teacher who expresses such genuine concerns raises realistic points. That same teacher may be required to make sure his students read and understand *Romeo and Juliet*. Before mentioning the words of Shakespeare, the teacher could work toward those classic words with a short analysis of conflicts at school. Perhaps a chart is shown that reveals the number of discipline referrals written by teachers in the previous school year with a categorization showing the 10 most common misbehaviors and the number of referrals in each of those 10 categories. The teacher and the students could analyze the statistics and consider reasons why those conflicts with rules happened.

From that discussion the class could move toward a discussion of unspoken conflict within the school. Why do groups of students gather each morning, at lunch, and after school with the same people, at the same place, never noticing anyone else? Is it just everyone being part of the group they prefer, or are there some unspoken limitations on who associates with whom?

Then the teacher can begin the transition to conditions in England centuries ago when social classes did not interact with people of lower social position. The students know something about conflict, written rules, unspoken rules, and social status from their life experience. Ten minutes of discussion about what they know followed by a logical connection to what they will learn about *Romeo and Juliet* can increase the productivity of the work done on Shakespeare.

Jumping right into the text of *Romeo and Juliet* without any mental preparation; without tapping into student life experience; without making connections with the wholesome knowledge, talents, and interests of students and what they need to learn can limit what the teacher and the students achieve. Why omit the power of connection? Why not work toward academically valid writing that fascinates students by beginning with topics that already fascinate students?

Self. Himself. Herself. Themselves. What is one topic that teachers can be almost 100 percent certain that students have wholesome expertise on, knowledge about, interest in, and commitment to? The students themselves as groups, each student himself or herself individually. Students, and to some degree adults also, are on the journey of self-discovery, self-identity, and self-expression; however, each student knows a lot about herself or himself. Students know their likes, dislikes, interests, career interests, favorite music, unique characteristics or personality traits, achievements thus far in life, and difficulties and disappointments thus far in life, and students think about themselves.

Conversations with students may include general statements that the student responds to with an "I" reply. "That test we took last week was difficult, which tells you that the class is getting increasingly harder." A student might reply, "Yeah, I mean, my grade was really low. I guess I just had a bad day."

"Did you hear what the president announced last night in his speech?" A student could reply, "I could do a better job as president than he does." Or "No, I had to work last night. My job is so crazy. My boss thinks we should clean the restaurant all the time. Everything has to shine. I need to find another job."

Some students are very involved in service activities ranging from environmental projects at the school campus to local, national, or international mission outreach projects sponsored by their church. The point of being aware of the fairly common student "I reply" is not to indict all students as being selfish or egocentric; rather it is to remind educators that the life experience, the personality, the thoughts, the likes or dislikes, the self of each student all combine to provide an abundance of resources to which the school curriculum can connect.

The presence of such personal connections in the classroom can help create personal commitment to learning by students who make minimal or no commitment to school. Also, this can help strengthen personal commitments from students who already seek success at school. Some dedicated students do not always see any personal meaning in schoolwork other than the importance of good grades because of what those grades provide now and can help attain later.

The following writing, thinking, creating, analyzing, and researching activities have been used in recent years with the high school juniors and seniors whom I taught. The results were very favorable for several reasons, including the following: (1) These activities were designed with my students in mind. With some of their wholesome knowledge, talents, and interests identified, these activities incorporated extreme writing concepts from the start; (2) The students often have choices in the topics they select and in the format they select—each choice they may consider is academically valid, as it is part of the curriculum; (3) These activities are not generic reruns from decades earlier in my career. These activities were designed for current students whose wholesome knowledge, talents, and interests are unique.

The intention of the case-study writing activity about the Great Depression was to put students who are 16 years old in the year 2009 into the realities of the 1929–1940 era. The students are interested in money, jobs, cars, food, and their family, so these case studies emphasized the human ordeal, agony, and crisis of survival that the Great Depression imposed on people. It is important to know the statistics of the Great Depression. It is impactful to feel how those statistics reflected day-to-day changes in how individuals lived.

## EXTREME WRITING ACTIVITY I

### U.S. History—The Great Depression Case Study

1. It is November 3, 1929. The stock you bought two years ago for $200 was paid for with $20 of your money and with $180 you borrowed. One month ago the stock was worth $1,500. Today it is worth $40. You had paid back only $48 of the $180 you borrowed so you still owe _____. You sell the stock for $40. You use that to pay back some of your debt, but even after that you still owe _____.

2. You work in Michigan for the Ford Motor Company and you get paid well. Even with the Model T Ford you bought last year and pay $3 per week on, and the big radio you bought that you pay $2 for each week, and the new refrigerator that you pay $2 for each week, you think you can pay your stock debt in a year or two.

    Problem: In 1929 the Ford Motor Company is not selling as many cars as in 1928. Seventy-five thousand Ford workers are laid off, and you are one of those workers. Now what will you do?

3. You decide to go to the bank and get your money out of your savings account, but you decide to wait until next week to do that because you are going to look for a new job first. You begin to hear rumors of problems at your bank, so you go there sooner than you planned. There is a very long line of people at the bank. The new rumor is that the bank is running out of money. With 46 people still in front of you, the bank door is closed and locked. The bank is out of business; it is bankrupt. You had $213 in your savings account. It is gone.

4. Apples. You heard that the apple growers have surplus apples. You can get some apples on credit, sell them for 5 cents each, and make some money. Other people have the same idea, so after one week of selling apples you have sold only 20 per day, a total of 100 this

week. That means you took in $5 but you have to pay back $2.50 for the apples you got from the farmer. You have made $2.50 this week. You used to make a lot more when you worked for Ford.

5. Now what? You decide to move to Kansas, where you have some family and they have a farm. You, your wife, and your three children pack up everything and head to Kansas. Conditions are not good, but at least the farm keeps everyone busy and fed, until the drought and the wind, and then the soil is gone; it is just gone. Now what?

Students are interested in money. Perhaps they have been told by their families that a car, a vacation, a new computer, some new clothes do not fit in the family budget. Perhaps they have begun to realize that continuously increasing college costs will price higher education much higher than their family can afford.

Students in U.S. History classes begin to notice that from time to time the nation has a financial panic, recession, or depression. Far beyond the typical business cycle, these financial difficulties are often caused by the same old mistakes made over and over. These mistakes, the students notice, include excessive credit and excessive speculation. The following extreme writing activity is designed to connect the wholesome interest that students have in money and the lessons that history can teach a nation or an alert student about sensible financial management. The next writing activity was designed with those objectives in mind.

## EXTREME WRITING ACTIVITY 2

### Lessons from U.S. Economic History

1920s
   a. Stocks were purchased on the speculation that high prices would continue to go higher.
   b. Stocks were purchased by some investors "on margin," meaning that some of the money used for the purchase was borrowed money.

   c. Consumer credit/borrowing increased through use of "install-
       ment plans" where weekly or monthly payments enabled people
       to get a new appliance or a new car now and pay over time.
   d. There were significant tax cuts for very wealthy people under
       the "trickle-down" theory.
   e. The stock market crashed in October 1929, and the Great De-
       pression began.
1980s
   a. Supply-side economics—this is a new name for trickle-down—
       brought a 25 percent reduction in income taxes with the tax cuts
       skewed toward wealthy people.
   b. The national government saw unprecedented deficits as spend-
       ing increased while government revenue never matched spend-
       ing levels.
   c. The Savings and Loan Crisis required a national government
       bailout.
   d. In October 1987 the stock market dropped about 20 percent in
       one day.
2000s
   a. Return of supply-side economics with large tax cuts in 2001.
       This followed two years in the late 1990s when the national gov-
       ernment had surpluses and was projecting that those surpluses
       could continue with significant reduction in the national debt.
   b. The 2001 tax cuts skewed toward wealthy people, again using a
       trickle-down theory.
   c. The national government began running unprecedented deficits.
   d. The mortgage, banking, and investing crisis of 2007–2008 con-
       tinues to impact the national economy with no lasting improve-
       ment anticipated soon.
   e. During October 2007–July 2008 the stock market has dropped
       in value 20 percent.
   f. Home foreclosures have been at very high rates in 2007 and
       2008.
   g. Unemployment worsened during 2008.

• Do you notice any pattern? Explain that.
• Do you notice any associated actions and results? Explain that.

- What lessons could be learned from these historical results?
- What's a citizen to do?
  a. Save, save more, keep saving.
  b. Avoid debt.
  c. Plan and save for your retirement. Expect nothing from Social Security. If you get anything from Social Security, treat it like a bonus.
  d. Get very serious about eliminating debt—personal, family, national.
  e. What other wise actions can be taken?

The study of U.S. history shares a content challenge with many other subjects—there is more to study and more to learn than the time in a school year allows. The math teacher who spends extra weeks on fractions may find insufficient time for the study of other required math skills. The science teacher who spends extra time on the solar system may find too little time for other required science topics. Time management is increasingly vital as the body of human knowledge increases while the length of the school year does not increase.

Projects such as the U.S. history magazine activity shown below can help with time management as each student researches several topics. This activity applies the extreme writing approach, as students may select topics from a long list so they match their wholesome interests or talents with the content of their magazine. The extreme writing approach also involves each student applying the insights of history to the real lives being lived today by the student and by readers of the magazine.

## EXTREME WRITING ACTIVITY 3

### U.S. History—1800–1860 Project:
### People, Events, Ideas

Research in library: Tuesday, September 25, 2007
Due: Tuesday, October 2, 2007
G-rated, legal, ethical
  1. Design a magazine with a title that communicates a theme and include the following parts in your magazine: (a) front cover; (b)

table of contents; (c) ads on the inside front cover, inside back cover, and back cover; (d) at least six articles, at least two of which are your original writing; (e) letters to the editor. Cite sources used in standard bibliography form.

2. Other formats: talk to me about what you create, and we will agree on it. The same amount of content would be included.

3. Two people could work together: (a) put in writing who did what and (b) in 1(d), change six to twelve, and each person writes two articles, indicating who wrote what.

4. A letter from the editor—that is you—explaining how the topics in this issue of your magazine provide ideas and guidance that you and the magazine readers can apply now.

The following are some of the topics that could be combined into a magazine with a theme you create, although other topics are possible:

War of 1812
Manifest Destiny
Henry Clay
Andrew Jackson
John C. Calhoun
Daniel Webster
Jacksonian Democracy
Canals
Steamboats
Roads
Turnpikes
Nullification
Erie Canal
1824 presidential election
Whig Party
Railroads
Aaron Burr
*Marbury v. Madison*
John Marshall
Women's Rights (including the 1848 Seneca Falls Convention)
Abolitionists

Henry David Thoreau
Ralph Waldo Emerson
Transcendentalists
Missouri Compromise of 1820
Mexican-American War
*Dred Scott* decision of the U.S. Supreme Court
Know-Nothing Party
1858 Lincoln-Douglas debates in Illinois
Reform movements
Second Great Awakening
Monroe Doctrine
Cotton gin
Telegraph
Sewing machine
Utopian communities
Shakers as in Shakertown in Mercer County, Kentucky
Underground Railroad
*Uncle Tom's Cabin*
Early history of the Democratic political party
Early history of the Republican political party
Early decades of the Industrial Revolution
McGuffey's Readers—schoolbooks
Trail of Tears

The reader will notice the repeated requirement on these writing projects that everything must be G-rated, legal, and ethical. That standard is nonnegotiable in what students say, write, or do in the classroom or for the class. Violations of that standard receive discipline action. Character education can be embedded in each classroom activity.

## EXTREME WRITING ACTIVITY 4

### The Twentieth Century in Pictures . . . and Words

Due: Monday, March 2, 2009; Everything is G-rated, legal, ethical
Choice of Major Topics: (a) 1901–1950 or (b) 1951–2000

Categories: listed below; if you think of others that are of interest and historically valid, discuss those with me.

Music
Architecture
Art
Literature
Transportation
Fashion
Media—radio, television, movies, newspapers, newsmagazines, electronic
Medicine and health
Aviation
Businesses, finances, and economics
Politics
Constitutional amendments
Sports
War
Inventions and technology
Fads
Your career interest

1. Select the major topic you prefer to investigate: (a) 1901–1950 or (b) 1951–2000.
2. Select five categories that are of most interest to you.
3. Get five pictures about each of the five categories from the time period you selected and arrange them on a page or on pages with the category identified/introduced.
4. Write a short caption about each picture—your original words/ writing.
5. Write a paragraph about each category—your original words/ writing.
6. Conclude with one page that describes the major topic based on what the pictures tell—your original words/writing.
7. Captions, paragraphs, and page are typed.
8. Yes, you can get creative in format, style, and design.

Students know how to communicate in many ways. Talking and electronic messages may be the two communication methods that students prefer. Writing does not make the top two ranking, at least not at first glance. Electronic messages are a form of writing. What people talk about could become the basis for writing. The next extreme writing activity applies those preferred student communication methods with the school curriculum to create another academically valid writing experience with the potential to fascinate.

## EXTREME WRITING ACTIVITY 5

### Advanced Placement U.S. History— April 2009 Project—Due: 4/27/09

G-rated, legal, ethical—words, pictures, everything

Topic: your choice of any major U.S. history event, idea, or person from 1946–2009. By Thursday, April 9, talk with me about your topic so we agree on it.

- Talk with—in person, by phone, by e-mail—two or more people whom you and/or your family know. These two or more people are selected because they have life experience and/or memory that can give you some personal perspective and information about the topic you select.

- Read—at least two quality sources to get accurate historical factual information about the topic. One source may be from the Internet, but that is not required. Use a reputable, accurate, reliable Internet source. The other source (sources if you use more than two) must be a book or another publication. Cite all sources properly.

- Write—two to three pages typed, double spaced, with 12-point font, that present your research with emphasis on what was learned through the interviews. Include (a) a short introduction; (b) the research findings, including verbatim quotes from the people you talk with; and (c) a conclusion that includes a short summary of what was learned and your reflection on what was learned. Different formats with the same amount of research, writing, and thinking are possible—talk to me about any format idea you are interested in other than the essay format.

- Cite the sources—With books or other printed material, cite in proper research format. If you use a website, cite it fully and include an explanation of why that was the best website to use. For people, ask each person if it is okay to mention them by name. You could refer to them in other ways, such as by their profession (*an attorney* remembered that), by number (*the first person* I talked to), or in terms of the topics (one person *who remembered attending a war protest*).
- Due—Monday, April 27, 2009, at the start of your class period. Having this done on time, completely, and correctly is the only way to get full credit. One hundred points possible.

Consider these words spoken by a high school junior: "If you can understand it with your life, you can understand it better." Those words were spoken on a Friday afternoon in October 2007 by one very active and insightful participant in a student-begun, student-led Christian club that, at the request of students, I sponsored for a year. Among the many benefits I was given through that volunteer work was to hear the idea quoted above. The student was speaking about the Bible. The student's wisdom has many applications, including to extreme writing.

The next set of extreme writing examples also uses the power of choice, which means that each student can complete the academic requirements while also individually customizing his or her work. This enables each student to do research, thinking, creating, and writing that their ideas, knowledge, talents, and interests helped shape, while meeting all academic requirements of each project.

As Dr. Earl Reum said when he taught a generation of student leaders some years ago: "People support what they help create." Yes, the teacher is in charge. Yes, the teacher is responsible for implementing lessons that match the curriculum. Yes, teachers can include the wholesome knowledge, talents, and interests of students as resources in the classroom learning process. There is no one perfect teaching method that will maximize the achievement of each student and eliminate all educational problems; however, making real connections between what students are already committed to, knowledgeable about, interested in, and talented in has obtained good results since Socrates asked sequential questions and since Jesus taught with parables.

## EXTREME WRITING ACTIVITY 6

### Political Science—October 2008 Project—
### The 2008 Presidential Election

Everything is G-rated, legal, ethical

Due: Tuesday, October 7, 2008, at the start of class; printed, stapled, your name on it. Have separate notes for your summary presentation to our class.

1. Talk with a variety of 10 registered voters and ask these questions:
   a. If the presidential election were held today, whom would you vote for?
   b. What are the strongest reasons that will cause you to vote for that candidate?
   c. Which presidential candidate are you most against?
   d. What are the strongest reasons for your opposition to that candidate?
   e. What are the two most important issues facing the nation today?
   f. What would you like to see a president accomplish on those two issues?
   g. Overall, what is your impression of the campaign for president so far?
   h. How do you evaluate the presidency of George W. Bush?
   i. What are the reasons that cause you to have that evaluation of President Bush?
   j. One other question you think of that relates to this topic.
2. 2.5 to 4.0 pages typed, double spaced, 12-point print. Include overall conclusions, some verbatim comments, and your reflections on and analysis of what you heard people say. Include a one-paragraph description of your research "sample," meaning the people you talked with. You do not have to identify anyone by name; in fact, let people know that if they prefer not be mentioned by name, that is fine. You could include a chart, table, or other data presentation.
3. Read some current polling data, such as what you can get from quality Internet sites about politics. What is similar about and/or

different with those polling numbers and what people told you? Begin now to monitor polls daily. Watch for any changes and update the figures. You could include a "tracking chart" showing daily numbers. Figure out what has caused those changes. Include some polling statistics and include your analysis of what those numbers are telling you.

4. Predictions: who will win the presidential election in November 2008? Explain the major fact/reason/evidence that causes you to say that person will win.

5. Yes, you may design a different format than pages of text. Yes, it is due on Tuesday, October 7, 2008—be here, turn it in on time, give us a one-minute summary in class of what your research told you.

## EXTREME WRITING ACTIVITY 7

### Political Science "Welcome to 2013" Project

Due: Monday, March 3, 2008—typed, G-rated, legal, ethical

Welcome to May 2013. Soon it will be time for the fifth reunion of your high school class of 2008. Let's think about the years 2008–2013.

1. Who was the Republican candidate for president of the United States in 2008? Explain several reasons why that person was chosen to be their candidate.

2. Who was the Democratic candidate for president of the United States in 2008? Explain several reasons why that person was chosen to be their candidate.

3. What were the three major issues in the general election campaign for president of the United States in 2008?

4. Who won the election for president of the United States in 2008? Explain how and why that person won. Also, were there any significant third-party candidates, and if so, what impact did they have? If there were no significant third-party candidates, explain why.

5. Write the opening paragraph and the closing paragraph, and list the three major points made by the new president in the inaugural address given in January 2009.

6. What were the two most important actions taken or decisions made by the new president in January 2009 and February 2009? Why were those top priorities?
7. Who was the Republican candidate for president of the United States in 2012? Explain several reasons why that person was chosen to be their candidate.
8. Who was the Democratic candidate for president of the United States in 2012? Explain several reasons why that person was chosen to be their candidate.
9. Who won the presidential election of 2012? Explain several reasons why that person won.
10. Now, think about you and what you experience and accomplish during 2008–2013. You may prefer to think of each year separately or of the five years together. Where were you during this time and what were you doing—school, work, military, job training, volunteer work, or other endeavors? What goals did you set and reach? What opportunities came your way? What challenges did you overcome? What are your plans for beyond 2013?

## EXTREME WRITING ACTIVITY 8

### Political Science

Due: Wednesday, January 14, 2009
Select one of the following topics:
1. Department of Defense
2. Department of State
3. Department of Treasury
4. Department of Justice
5. Department of Interior
6. Department of Agriculture
7. Department of Commerce
8. Department of Labor
9. Department of Health and Human Services
10. Department of Housing and Urban Development
11. Department of Transportation

12. Department of Energy
13. Department of Education
14. Department of Veterans Affairs
15. Department of Homeland Security
16. Federal Deposit Insurance Corporation
17. Environmental Protection Agency
18. Hoover Commission (first and/or second)
19. Grace Commission
20. Kentucky state government—departments; constitutional officers
21. Lexington, Kentucky, local government—departments, elected officials
22. Merger of Lexington and Fayette County governments

Do:
1. The history of the department, agency, other
2. The mission, duties, authority, jurisdiction of the department, agency, other
3. The current budget of the department, agency, other—trends in recent years
4. Benefits and services provided to citizens by the department, agency, other
5. Achievements that stand out made by the department, agency, other
6. What seemed most interesting to you
7. A recommendation you would suggest that this department, agency, other make
8. Give us a summary of your research

Format: lots of choices—poster, text, charts, graphs, tables, pages/paragraphs, creativity

## EXTREME WRITING ACTIVITY 9

### Political Science Project, Chapters 18 and 19 or Chapters 20 and 21

Due: Wednesday, March 4, 2009, at 10:32 A.M., done completely, correctly, and ready to hand in, including already stapled and your name is on it

Create your version of chapters 18 and 19 or chapters 20 and 21. Include the following:

 a. A title for the new chapter.
 b. An introduction of the chapter.
 c. A list of essential vocabulary for the chapter—(1) terms, (2) the
    meaning of each term, and (3) an explanation of what is impor-
    tant about each term.
 d. Four case studies—court cases, interviews, political activity,
    campaign speeches, position papers, debates, other—that deal
    with topics of chapters 18 and 19 or chapters 20 and 21.
 e. Text—your words and some other materials not from our text-
    book; include charts, graphs, quotes, tables, illustrations.
 f. A conclusion/summary of the chapter.
 g. A quiz about the chapter—at least 10 questions.
 h. A test about the chapter—include two essay questions.
 i. An evaluation that tells why—three or more detailed reasons—
    your version of chapters 18 and 19 or chapters 20 and 21 is bet-
    ter than the textbook version. Explain specific contrasts.
 j. A separate page that lists all sources used in proper notation
    form. Use reputable, accurate, reliable, sophisticated, intel-
    lectual sources—think tanks, interest groups, government sites,
    respected print publications and their online versions. Include
    at least two books other than our textbook.

## EXTREME WRITING ACTIVITY 10

Due: Thursday, March 13; G-rated, legal, ethical
Ready to hand in at the start of class. Typed. Stapled. Name on it.
    Ready at the moment class begins. That's how it works in college,
    so get in that habit now and stay in that habit.
 1. You were given a list of 12 political issues that, as a class, you
    said yesterday were important to you. Select one political issue
    that especially interests you. Do not select the two issues we will
    discuss this week in class: fair tax and term limits.
 2. In your words and in one or two paragraphs for each point
    below:
    a. Explain and summarize the pro side.
    b. Explain and summarize the con side.

    c. Include verbatim two to four quotes from an article to pro-
       vide the strongest reasons for the pro side.

    d. Include verbatim two to four quotes from an article to pro-
       vide the strongest reasons for the con side.

3. What is your opinion on the issue? Pick one of the following
options and explain why, using two or three reasons you think
that way.

    a. Pro

    b. Con

    c. Other, such as "hybrid," meaning truth is a blend or in the
       middle

4. If you were debating a person who thinks differently from you
on this topic

    a. What would be the strongest reason, point, or idea that per-
       son could make?

    b. What would you say to persuasively refute that strong point?

5. Find, cite the source of, and quote three additional sources to
support your side

    a. A presidential candidate or other person in politics now

    b. An interest group or other relevant organization

    c. A person or group not directly involved in politics

6. Explain two or three actions you could take now to support your
side.

7. Five years from now, what will be the status of this issue? Why?

8. In class on March 13, give us a one- or two-minute summary of
your findings.

The 10 extreme writing activities shown above are not intended to
be copied and used as they are; rather, they are to become the starting point for each reader to now think about those 10 activities and
create Extreme Writing Activity 11. An idea or an inspiration may be
applied from activities 1 through 10, but those were designed for my
students based on their unique strengths and goals; on their knowledge, talents, and interests; and on the curriculum of our school,
school district, and state.

The connection to the curriculum makes the activities academically
valid. The connection to the students' real lives they are living right now

makes the activities relevant. The connection to the students' wholesome knowledge, interests, and talents makes the activities personally meaningful and individually unique. The choices of topics and formats help build commitment and meaning. The whole process creates extreme learning through extreme writing.

Now it is your turn. First, think of a specific objective for a lesson in which a writing activity could be used as one of the ways students will master the objective. Second, think of the exact way you intend to use writing as part of that lesson. Third, think of how you can design that writing to be extreme writing that connects what needs to be learned with the wholesome knowledge, interests, and talents of students. Fourth, design the extreme writing activity.

Here's an example:

1. Lesson plan objective: to understand why and to explain why eating healthy foods from each food group is more nutritious than eating healthy food from only one food group.
2. Why and how a writing activity will be used: to build awareness of the idea that there is strength in variety. Write a compare-and-contrast paper.
3. How connections will be incorporated in the writing activity: students will realize the essential importance of variety in music, sports, television, and cars.
4. The exact extreme writing activity: Describe and evaluate one of the following: (a) the impact on a school band if trumpet is the only instrument any band member is allowed to play; (b) the impact on a basketball team if only one player is allowed to take shots in a game; (c) the impact on your television viewing if only one station/network existed; and (d) the impact on driving if only one car company existed and they manufactured only one model of one brand of a car. Then (e) write three to five paragraphs in which you compare and contrast the topic chosen in part 4 with the idea of the food pyramid that has been discussed in class.

Now you have read an example, so it is your turn. Think of your curriculum and your students so the activity you create can be used in your classroom.

1. Lesson plan objective:
2. Why and how a writing activity will be used:
3. How connections will be incorporated in the writing activity:
4. The exact extreme writing activity:

The answer to the emerging question from the reader is "no." What is the question? "Do I have to consult the curriculum; create a rationale for writing; list the wholesome knowledge, talents, and interests of students and select a few of these for connections with each activity; and then design the exact extreme activity?" What supports a "no" answer?

You already know the curriculum. You know the types of and purposes of writing activities including these types: one paragraph; a page; a list of ideas; a formal paper; to introduce a new concept; to analyze; to compare and contrast; to explain; to describe.

Some thinking and planning are required, but there are efficiencies, such as know the curriculum thoroughly; know the most effective uses for writing activities in your classes; know the wholesome knowledge, interests, and talents of your students. The more thoroughly, deeply, and accurately you know those topics, the more efficiently you can design extreme writing activities.

Please notice that your development of a thorough, deep, and accurate (1) knowledge of the curriculum; (2) experience with and evaluation of the writing and other instructional activities that get the best results with and for your students; and (3) awareness of the wholesome knowledge, talents, and interests of students will equip you to both design extreme writing activities and to create an extreme writing atmosphere in the classroom. In all of your interaction with students in your classes for note taking, for discussion, for analysis of materials read, the thinking and resulting writing can include connections between what students already know and what students need to know.

## FOR TEACHERS ONLY: TEACHING INSIGHT 7

What is your opinion of lesson plans? What is your opinion of lesson planning?

Planning is essential. Coaches write a game plan. Corporate executives have a business plan. Advertisers have a media plan.

Teachers who plan their day-to-day objectives and instructional activities benefit from the thinking that goes into planning and from the structure the plan gives to time management, priorities, and implementation of the curriculum. Results are enhanced when each day is part of an overall plan for the year. The daily specifics help create the yearly results.

The goal is to cause learning, not to create the ultimate lesson plan that conforms to all Department of Lesson Plan Perfection requirements. An apparently perfect, as it appears on paper, lesson plan may or may not actually work in the classroom. The measurement of the lesson plan is in the learning that was caused as the lesson was implemented.

When a school administrator begins requiring long, detailed lesson plans that consume much time, perhaps the administrator is being pressured from higher in the chain of command or perhaps the administrator is convinced that what looks good on paper must work well in the classroom.

Somewhere between no lesson plans and severe micromanagement via intricately detailed, almost scripted, lesson plans is a reasonable midpoint where the teacher has a written lesson plan to guide productive work and to inform administrators who need that information. Quality lesson planning is essential. Bureaucratic lesson-plan micromanagement can be counterproductive. Teachers and administrators who reason together on lesson plans can find a sensible system that enhances instruction, helps cause learning, and helps administrators have some information about and a written record of part of what is being done day to day in all classrooms. Still, there is a better way to know about instruction throughout a school, as described below.

## FOR PRINCIPALS ONLY: ADMINISTRATOR INSIGHT 4

Visit classrooms. Visit classrooms often. Visit classrooms for complete class periods.

Lesson plans provide a written summary of the objective for and the activities of a class. To fully know about the lesson requires being there.

You cannot be in every classroom during every class period of every day. You can visit as much as you make it a priority to visit. A lesson plan is a recipe. Visiting the classroom for the entire class is consuming the food the recipe designed.

Situations occur daily at schools that only the administrators can resolve. Those discipline matters, building concerns, meetings, people who come to school expecting to see the principal right now, hallway supervision, cafeteria supervision, and more can seem to control and can easily consume all of your time unless you intentionally control your time.

Go to classrooms. Do not stay in a classroom for three minutes and claim to know what that class was about. Watching three minutes of a sporting event, concert, or movie cannot provide a full appreciation of or awareness of the entire event. Treat classrooms as well as or better than people treat sporting events, concerts, or movies.

If you do make quick visits to classrooms, do not use those "snapshots" as the basis for broad conclusions. That is not a valid basis, as you learned in research classes.

When you see a teacher working with students on a writing activity, know that planning had to happen first and that grading the papers will take time and effort by the teacher after class. Be sure to acknowledge that extra time if you discuss with the teacher the part of class you observed.

Instructional leadership requires instructional awareness, which requires being there. To do less is to be merely an instructional supervisor or, worse, an instructional clerk. The pushes and pulls on your time will take you away from classrooms unless you push harder and pull harder to get into classrooms.

---

Imagine that a class is discussing a presidential inaugural speech and a student who is very interested in movies comments that the speech and a scene from a certain film were similar. The teacher could lead a discussion about the similarities and differences in preparing, rehearsing, staging, presenting, and evaluating a presidential inaugural address and in creating a scene for a movie. Notes could be put on the board as the discussion continues—these notes are in the extreme writing category, as they show connections. Then each student could be asked to write a paragraph that evaluates which task is simpler—for a president to present a superior inaugural address or for an actor to present a superior monologue in a movie?

As the unexpected extreme writing moments emerge in a classroom, the alert extreme writing teacher will maximize such opportunities. The students will have become comfortable with and successful with the formal, planned extreme writing approach, so as this approach expands into the informal or unplanned moments of connections in class, the students and the teacher can easily maximize the opportunities. (The three books *Extreme Teaching*, *Extreme Learning*, and *Extreme Students* provide details.)

The next chapter will take us from the general concept of and overall implementation of extreme writing to the subject-specific uniqueness that extreme writing can provide within each subject taught in elementary school, middle school, or high school. Before moving to the next chapter we will visit a teacher whose classroom experience shows how an extreme writing educational experience can be available at some spontaneous moments and can fit perfectly within the curriculum.

## CASE STUDY 5

"You know, every class I take at this school has tons of writing. It was that way in ninth grade and tenth grade. This year is the worst. Who decided that high school juniors had to write so much?"

The comment was genuine. Brian was a very conscientious, capable high school junior whose grades and other achievements at school were exemplary. He studied thoroughly for tests. He participated in class discussions. He turned in all assignments, on time. He completed all required summer reading, although whenever possible he listened to the books on his computer or phone instead of reading them. He said he learned and remembered more from listening to books instead of traditional reading.

Robert Alexander is a masterful high school teacher. His knowledge of chemistry and physics is sufficient to have led him into a lucrative research career for corporations or universities. He considered those options seriously, and at one point in college he leaned toward corporate research when some economics classes made him more aware of the possibilities for scientific achievement through corporate research. From new medications to new green energy products, Robert's scientific skills could certainly have been applied in the corporate arena.

Instead, he had decided to be a high school teacher. Why? He knew many adults who had various career experiences, but he never heard anyone discuss their career as one of his high school teachers discussed her work. Her science classroom was the most vibrant, interactive, challenging intellectual experience Robert had known during high school. He got the idea that he could do that same work and that he should do that same work. The idea grabbed his mind and heart relentlessly.

After 12 years of magnificent high school teaching results, Robert was certain he was doing the work he was supposed to do. Plus, most summers he did four or five weeks of intense research work at a nearby university through a high-school-to-college partnership.

The pay for that summer month was provided by a local company for which the university did research. One month in the summer of university and corporate research paid Robert the equivalent of four months of his teacher pay. He also got to employ two of his best high school students in the research work. It was the perfect summer job for a student who had just completed the junior year of high school. Robert's two scholars often were awarded full or almost-full scholarships from the same university. Those scholarships were funded by the same local corporation that had the research venture with the university.

Brian's comment about writing was taken seriously by Mr. Alexander, who had just handed out the next Chemistry class writing assignment. Brian's comment was the start of a productive discussion Mr. Alexander had not planned, but could tell immediately had benefits if guided strategically. Mr. Alexander replied to Brian.

"Excellent point, Brian, excellent point. Your high school does place a major emphasis on writing. Any other thoughts on this topic from anyone?"

Julie quickly raised her hand. She had discussed this topic with her friends often as they dealt with the amount of work their junior year included.

"I agree. We write all the time in every class. I know that we need to be good at writing. Our English teachers have worked on that since elementary school. I just don't see why Chemistry or Calculus or U.S. History has to be more about writing than about chemistry and stuff. We learn chemistry with our experiments and projects. Isn't chemistry something to do instead of something to write about?"

Several other students joined in the class discussion. "I'm fine with writing up to a point. If I have a writing assignment in every class at the same time, there is no way I'll get all of them done as well as if some classes used something else, you know, something that is not writing," said Angela.

Amy added a technology reason. "Pencils, pens, and paper are so old-fashioned. Everything I do is electronic, except some of the homework; well, actually, almost all of the homework and other work for school. Writing all of these things for school is like writing letters. Who does that anymore? We call or we text message. We use computers or cell phones, but in our classes we use pens and pencils and paper. Don't schools like the twenty-first century?"

Thomas explained another reason. "I work on the school newspaper. This year we are moving to only an electronic version. Sure, we still write the paper, but we publish it on the Internet. We almost never use pens or paper. We do everything electronically with laptop computers and digital cameras and stuff like that."

Mr. Alexander had an idea. "The assignment I just gave you includes some writing. The reason is that when you go from doing an experiment or other chemistry work to explaining it in written words, you have to think in very exact ways. Words do that, especially written words. So let's do this. You still have the assignment to take one day this week and keep a chemistry diary. Keep track of everything in your life that chemistry impacts or is part of, like the cereal you had for breakfast. What's chemistry got to do with that? Now, create a different format for presenting part of the diary. Some of the diary is in writing. Some of it can be pictures, photographs, computer graphics, or other creative options. The amount of work is the same, but how you do part of the work changes. Then include your evaluation of what you learned and experienced with the two different methods. Any questions?"

Brian had a question. "If we impress you with what we learn, could you ask our other teachers to give us choices like this?"

Mr. Alexander smiled as he said, "I can share this idea with the faculty. Sure, Brian, we'll publish our results so all teachers can benefit. Now, back to our topic for today. Where and how does chemistry get used in this school building? Similar to the diary you'll keep of chemistry in your typical 24-hour activities, where do we find chemistry applied at school?"

When the chemistry diaries were turned in, Mr. Alexander eagerly graded them. The students included a lot of writing that just seemed to be in keeping with a diary. Each student also used pictures, drawings, posters, computer graphics, computer-assisted design pages, and fictional stories with illustrations, bringing chemistry applications to life in animated form. When Mr. Alexander returned the projects, he led a discussion about how chemistry showed up everywhere all day in the life of each student. He also led a discussion about the formats used to collect and present the diaries. Julie had an overall observation that seemed to match the experiences of just about everyone in the class.

"No matter what format we used, writing was still part of it. Even the pictures people used had descriptions in words included. We realized that chemistry is everywhere, and maybe we realized that writing in one form or another is everywhere."

It was right for Brian to get in the last comment, since this topic began with his original statement. "Teachers always tell me that text messages are just writing on a screen. I know that text messages are writing, but I would never send those messages on paper. My project did show me that I kept using writing, but when Thomas and I text messaged each other whenever we found another example of chemistry in everyday life, it just made it more interesting. So if the chemistry book can somehow become lots of little text messages, it will be perfect."

Mr. Alexander's imagination responded positively to that idea. The issue was not so much having to write. The students had realized that no matter what format they used, writing was essential. Now, if the pen, paper, pencil versus electronic screen divide could be bridged, the results could be unlimited.

Writing will endure. Writing is a unique process of thinking, becoming expressed, becoming manifested, becoming tangible, becoming structured, and becoming three-dimensional. Pens, pencils, paper or keyboards, screens, electronics? The common bond is thinking becoming written expression. Robert would maintain the academic integrity and standards to challenge high school chemistry students. There would be times when only pen, pencil, and paper would evoke the required work. Other times would permit a range of formats.

To Robert this continuous development of the best way to teach the current students was part of what challenged him as a teacher. He continually learned about how to most effectively teach what is known now about chemistry to students in high school now. Learning knows no limits in Mr. Alexander's classroom, where extreme writing within the science curriculum is a perpetual work in progress that inspires students to perpetually make progress.

# 5

# WRITING ACROSS THE CURRICULUM; WRITING WITHIN THE CURRICULUM

Trends. Fads. Jargon. Acronyms. Education has been known to eagerly and with good intentions chase the most recent trend, follow the newest fad, speak with peculiar jargon known only to insiders, and fill sentences with acronyms that require a glossary to comprehend.

"Writing across the curriculum will be emphasized in a pilot program for all ninth-graders. This will be part of a differentiated instruction initiative mandated by Central Office in response to a state department of education investigation of allegations that IEP implementation was incomplete, that GT programs were insufficiently individualized, and that some NCLB requirements were not adequately addressed as required in a smaller learning communities grant."

What does that mean? It suggests, after translation from educational jargon and acronyms, that a school is using writing in each subject as a way to implement a program to individualize teaching methods rather than have the exact same task being done by each student in a class despite the range of academic skills and needs in that class. This also suggests concerns about implementation of individual education plans (IEPs) related to the special education program; concerns about individualization of educational opportunities for students in the gifted and talented program (GT), or about whether GT work was actually being implemented; concerns about meeting requirements of the No Child Left Behind law; and further concerns about meeting requirements of a grant that had been awarded to the school.

## FOR PRINCIPALS ONLY: ADMINISTRATOR INSIGHT 5

Public laws impact public education. It is common for the law of public education to be included in the classes educators take in the process of earning certification to be an administrator. It is less common for those classes to include guidance on how to impact the political process of lawmaking.

The Tenth Amendment to the U.S. Constitution can be understood by reasonable people to mean that the national government has no constitutional authority to get involved in education. States and local governments, especially school districts, have authority over education. The U.S. Constitution does not include the word *school* or the word *education*.

School administrators can stand up for local and state control of education. The national government cannot micromanage the nation's schools and classrooms.

The extreme writing approach works at the classroom level because a teacher effectively implements activities that connect what students know, are talented in, or are interested in and what they need to learn through writing. The national government cannot accomplish that.

School administrators, perhaps working through professional associations of principals or superintendents, can resist the Washington, D.C., manipulative temptation of a minor part of school funding that comes at the cost of Washington, D.C., attempting to impact major parts of what schools do.

Education progress happens in classrooms and in schools, not through Congress or the White House. School administrators can help keep school control local by resisting national government invasions of schools. By avoiding the national government's bureaucratic complications of paperwork, tests, reports, forms, and regulations, schools can emphasize teaching and learning. Teachers need school administrators to shield them from the social engineering that the national government is inclined to attempt to accomplish through schools.

State and local governments do have constitutional authority over education; however, alert school administrators will be vigilant in dealing with the state or local education bureaucracy. The state government that passes a law dealing with "all students will master reading and writing skills required at each grade level before moving to the next grade level" is in pursuit of an honorable goal; however, reaching that goal will rely on what teachers do in classrooms. School administrators can ensure that state and local governments continuously hear the classroom reality that only teachers can provide so laws and policies are reality based.

---

The reality in education is that of all the factors educators can control, the factor that most impacts student achievement is what happens in the classrooms between teachers and students. Any trend or fad in education that attempts to perfect the educational experience through (1) bureaucratic reforms, (2) scripted lesson plans, (3) social engineering, (4) federal government invasion of schools in defiance of the Tenth Amendment of the U.S. Constitution, (5) changing political priorities, pressures, or whims in state governments, (6) school board initiatives based only on a presentation at a national conference about what allegedly worked well at another very different school district, (7) or similar "disconnected from classroom reality" initiatives will not get the desired results.

In recent years or decades much emphasis has been given to the concept of and to the use of "writing across the curriculum." The rationale seemed to be "writing is important, so every student will write in every class." One result, perhaps an unintended consequence, was some contrived writing activities that were not designed to maximize learning, but were used to satisfy a bureaucratic requirement to have at least one writing activity per class weekly.

In music class the best activity could be to sing. In art class the best activity could be to draw. In physical education class the best activity could be physical activity. In math class the priority could be completing math problems to confirm mastery of math skills and concepts. The priority in science class could be to successfully design, implement, and analyze experiments. In English class reading may be the priority, or perhaps it is character analysis or vocabulary development. In world history class biographical information or historical data may be given high priority.

Still, if the bureaucratic, political, legal, regulatory management structure required "writing across the curriculum," the teachers would stop the drawing in art classes so students could write about drawing, and the physical education teachers would stop the softball game so students could write about softball, and the math teacher would have to require that students explain how to solve a math problem even if the teacher knew the students had not yet mastered that type of math problem.

Writing is good. Writing puts ideas into words. Writing helps ideas take form, shape, structure, and life. Writing tests and clarifies and develops thinking. The goodness of writing is not a reason to abandon or to deemphasize other learning activities that can be equally effective in some circumstances and for some students could be more effective.

Writing is good. When the most productive way to teach the current learning objective is writing, then writing should be used. The writing done about the rules of softball or the rules of adding fractions will be more productive if students have read the rules and played softball within those rules or have attempted some math problems with fractions and have manipulated some tangible pieces of plastic or wood to feel, to see, to discover what fractions do when they are physically combined. From the physical experience of softball or of fractions could come intellectual understanding that is followed by insightful writing.

Apples are a nutritious food, but complete nutrition requires more than apples. Running is effective exercise, but complete physical fitness requires more than running. Having a bank savings account is important for financial success, but complete financial planning requires more than a savings account. Writing is a very effective teaching method, but it is not the only effective teaching method. Writing can help cause learning, but writing is not the only way to cause learning, and writing will not by itself cause complete learning by all students of all parts of the curriculum.

What's a teacher to do when the writing across the curriculum trend mandates more and more writing? Use your professional judgment, take a professional stand, be the voice of classroom reality, and tell the bureaucracy or the fad followers or the policy makers (1) that in classrooms one-size instruction does not fit all educational needs, abilities, or objectives for all students; (2) that great teachers use a variety of teaching activities, techniques, and methods; (3) to take advice from doctors who diagnose a patient and who prescribe treatment for that patient rather than using an "aspirin across the patient list" and giving aspirin to everyone no matter what actual medical condition any patient had; and (4) that students are real people living real lives right now.

The person who is face-to-face with students daily is the teacher; therefore, educational policy, law, regulation, and reform must include substantial input from teachers instead of substantial imposition, edicts, political power plays, or bureaucratic processes from people in the educational or political hierarchy who are not working all day, every day with students.

"Oh, no, it's Friday and we have not done any writing this week. I have to turn in samples of student writing after school today. It has to be writing done this week that matches this week's topics. I meant to have them write yesterday, but the lab work we did took more time than I expected and the students were so fascinated by that experiment. Does it make sense to not finish the experiment today just so we write something that I can turn in to the principal so she can mark my name off the list and tell her boss that every teacher used writing across the curriculum for the seventh consecutive week?"

Learning is a human process. Learning at school that has the deepest, the most profound, the most enduring, and the most endearing impact on students is caused by teachers who (1) use a variety of teaching methods, activities, and techniques; (2) challenge their students; (3) are enthusiastic about students, teaching, and learning; and (4) make connections between what students need to learn and the wholesome knowledge, talents, and interests of students. Those four factors have been identified and confirmed during the past 15 years as I have asked over 4,000 educators to tell me about the best teacher they ever had. In the past few years those four factors were further confirmed as I listened to several hundred high school seniors pay tribute to the best teacher they ever had.

There are no mysteries or secrets. We know what great teachers do. We also know that great teaching is not a function of or a result of bureaucratic procedures, national or state government education reform initiatives, new laws, new regulations, new policies, fads, or trends.

Great teachers cause learning through the very human process of knowing the curriculum, getting to know the students, and designing instructional activities that cause the current students to best learn the current curriculum. The four factors listed above are part of that very human process. Extreme writing can be part of that very human process. The part that extreme writing plays will vary from classroom to classroom depending on the reality of each classroom.

When extreme writing is the best way to teach the current curriculum portion that is the emphasis of today's lesson, use extreme writing. How extreme writing is used and when extreme writing is used will vary also from one subject to another subject, because subjects have uniqueness that bureaucracies may not fully realize, but that teachers and students realize is part of the daily classroom reality.

Bureaucracies mandate writing across the curriculum. Classroom reality replies that writing within each separate subject of the curriculum can work, yet with allowance for differences in how each subject is best taught, with further allowances for how each teacher determines to best teach each class, and with additional allowances for individualized learning experiences that will vary across the students in a classroom.

## WRITING WITHIN THE ELEMENTARY SCHOOL CURRICULUM

A fourth-grade teacher noticed that her students could easily use the computer to search for any geographical location in their city or state. They could use the same process for geographical locations nationally or internationally. The teacher's concern was that the geography curriculum included skills in identifying places, but also included skills in knowing how different places were located in terms of other places. Using a computer to locate London, England, and London, Kentucky, may show those two places, but may not help the student develop a sense of geographic scale or perspective.

Would a wall map help? Could a globe help? Maybe drawing a map of the world is one way to get a perspective on places and distances. Could talking to people who travel a lot be informative? What did the explorers have to learn about geography, and would a source such as the diaries of Columbus apply to this topic? Maybe space travel could be revealing and photographs of Earth from the space shuttle could be used.

The students could design a map of their classroom and then a map of the school building. Those maps could be part of establishing an overall mental picture of a place and then of expanding the mental-picture concept to a city, to various cities, and eventually to the planet.

Several of these activities were used with good results. The teacher knew that the students were developing some geographical awareness and perspective. She decided to use a writing task to more thoroughly apply and measure these emerging geography skills. The teacher was convinced there was an aspect of this topic that only writing could develop, apply, and measure.

"You know where you live. You know where our school is. You could go from your home to school by walking, by being driven in a car, or by riding a school bus. The routes you would take if you walked, rode in a car, or rode on a school bus would be different for various reasons. Describe the exact route you would use with each of the three transportation methods. Now think about what was done the same with each route and list what was the same. Then think about what was different for each route and list what was different. If you had your choice and your family approved, explain which method of getting to school you prefer and why. Give at least four reasons to support your choice."

Geography is not limited to information about continents, oceans, rivers, faraway places, or maps. Geography is as close as the route, the locations passed, and the details along the way as a student goes from home to school. Students have much knowledge about their neighborhood but may not have organized that knowledge in geographic terms and systems. Going from the neighborhood geography to geography anywhere can be much more logical, meaningful, personal, connected, and worthwhile than just jumping into chapter 1 of the geography book and answering the generic geography questions at the end of each section in the chapter.

The day arrives when the fourth-grade geography project is due. The students have completed the work with a sense of accomplishment, of pride, and of satisfaction. After all of the projects were turned in, the students were asked to give a short summary of what they had discovered about their neighborhood as they completed this assignment.

"I found out that the cars and my school bus go different ways. The car gets me here faster, but the bus can save energy, since it brings more people."

"I discovered that walking is the best way to get to school because you can notice a lot more when you walk."

"When you walk you can take a shortcut. The car and the bus have to go where streets go. It's like, I mean, it's like the people we studied in history who had to blaze a trail."

"I discovered that this was not easy to do, but that was okay because I got to make a big poster to show all of my information and, well, posters are cool and we aren't always allowed to make posters."

"Here's what I thought. Geography could make a great game, maybe for little children. They could play a board game about going all over their neighborhood in a car, on a bus, or walking. It would be an even better game, you know, if we add using a bicycle or a skateboard. I really think the first-graders or second-graders would like a game about geography."

For many reasons, students see life, school, and the world differently than teachers see the world. One reason is that students and teachers are in different age-groups. Another reason is that teachers have completed college, have a full-time job, and have the responsibilities of adulthood while the life experiences of students do not yet include college, full-time employment, or adulthood.

The way students do see life, school, and the world is essential for teachers to be aware of and is a potentially productive resource for teachers to use. What geography means to a teacher could include what the school's curriculum states that students will learn about geography. To a student who visited her aunt and uncle last summer in Denver, geography includes the Rocky Mountains, which she explored on a long hike with her aunt, uncle, and cousins. Each student has had some personal interaction with some aspect of geography, including their neighborhood.

Using what already makes sense to the brain as a way to enhance learning of something new conforms with how the brain works. The brain seeks to find connections. The brain uses what already makes sense, what it has already processed, what it has stored in memory; when something new is encountered, the brain checks to see what, if anything, in its mental storage can connect with the new information or the new stimulus it is encountering. Extreme writing applies this organizing process where the brain puts a premium on mental, intellectual, cognitive connections.

The fourth-grade student whose study of geography connected with and applied her knowledge of her neighborhood was able to extend this thinking to the idea of creating a geography board game. She knows her neighborhood, and that helped her learn about geography. She knows about board games, and that can help her apply or extend her learning about geography. Now she realizes that geography does not exist in isolation in a textbook at school; rather, geography is as real as her neighborhood and could be as creative as an enjoyable board game.

As other fourth-grade teachers hear about the good results the students had with the neighborhood geography extreme writing project, they might wonder how they could duplicate that writing project in math, science, or language arts classes. A more productive thought would be to analyze why the neighborhood geography activity got good results and to borrow from those insights. The goal is not to immediately create duplicate versions of neighborhood math, neighborhood science, or neighborhood language arts; rather, the goal is to cause learning.

Extreme writing does that by making connections between the wholesome knowledge, talents, and interests of students and what students need to learn. The neighborhood connection worked effectively as a basis for the geography writing activity. The extreme writing activity for math could be a set of connections between math skills and sport statistics, cooking recipe measurements, pizza servings, or counting coins.

The extreme writing activity for science could be a set of connections between science and how a car works, skateboard tricks or stunts, how exercise and nutrition help you get healthy and stay healthy, how weather conditions impact a scouting campout, or what similarities there are in travel by airplane and travel by spacecraft. What connections would the reader suggest for a fourth-grade language arts teacher to use in an extreme writing activity?

There is merit in using extreme writing to enhance learning of many elementary school subjects. Other teaching methods and activities should be used in addition to extreme writing. The total range of possible activities that pass the requirement of causing learning can create more quality of and more quantity of learning than exclusive reliance on only one activity. No matter what the type of activity, the use of connections can increase the effectiveness of the activity.

Of course, for extreme writing to work the students must have sufficient fundamental writing skills of vocabulary, sentence structure, use of punctuation, organization of paragraphs, and matching subjects with verbs. What extreme writing activity could be designed to help students master the fundamentals of proper writing? Perhaps connections with rules of a sport and rules of writing could work. Explain how soccer would be different if players could carry the ball with their hands. Now explain how writing would be different if each student decided how he or she would spell each word instead of using the authorized, standardized spelling system.

## WRITING WITHIN THE MIDDLE SCHOOL CURRICULUM

Middle school students are often organized into teaching teams. Let's visit an eighth-grade team meeting and hear from the four teachers on that team as they plan an interdisciplinary unit with the theme of exploration and with no established or mandated list of teaching methods that must be used. What is mandated is the curriculum, and during this unit each teacher has identified what he or she needs to emphasize in the school's approved sequence of studies. The teaching team members are Mr. Roberts, social studies; Ms. Bethel, language arts; Ms. Matthews, science; and Mr. Peterson, math. Ms. Bethel is the team leader.

Ms. Bethel:     Okay, let's get started. This is such a busy time. Progress reports will be printed next week, so all grades have to be in the computer by this Friday. We usually do a good job with keeping current on grades. The faculty meets next Tuesday right after school. Any other reminders? No. Okay; let's give the interdisciplinary unit some thought. The students selected the theme of exploration. We'll use this theme for the next two weeks. In language arts we need to work on short stories. There are several short stories we'll read that I chose for the exploration theme. I thought their big project would be to write their own short story about some exploration they have done or would like to do.

Ms. Matthews: That gives me an idea. The next big topic in science is how the body fights infection, illness, and disease. Maybe we could explore the path that infections take in the body and the path that our natural defense systems take to fight illnesses. I'd like to somehow decorate the room so it looks like the inside of a cell or of a vein or of a vital organ. That way no matter where the students look in the room, they are exploring part of the body that is related to fighting illness. My dream would be for the room to be like an amusement park ride that takes you throughout the circulatory system as antibodies chase and fight germs or toxins or something like that. Maybe students could create that kind of special effect in the classroom.

Mr. Roberts: Social studies and exploration sound like a good match, but for the next two weeks we're studying the Industrial Revolution. If we were on the westward movement or the space program, it sure would be a better fit. Maybe you can help me fit the Industrial Revolution into the exploration theme.

Mr. Peterson: Math is not much better, but it will work. The topic for the next two weeks is introduction to geometry. I always like geometry, and I could be fascinated with the exploration of different ways to do a geometric proof, but I'm not so sure that will work for all of my students. Okay. Now what do we do?

Ms. Bethel: Let's work backward. In two weeks, at the end of the exploration unit, what do we want the students to have learned? Take a minute and write down a very clear statement of your intended result for the students.

Ms. Matthews: I actually have several objectives. I organize the daily objectives to flow in a logical sequence. I really don't create a separate overall objective for a unit.

Ms. Bethel: Well, just see what you can come up with if you combine those daily objectives. We're not trying to create unnecessary work. We just want to be sure the exploration unit is productive and makes sense.

Ms. Matthews: Okay. How's this? Students will be able to describe how the human body fights against illnesses and diseases.

Students will know the vocabulary, the processes, what works, what goes wrong, and differences from one person to another as the human body tries to stay well. Is that okay? I was writing as I spoke, but it sounded good.

**Mr. Peterson:** Sounds good to me. My students will work on geometry. The overall objective is for students to show that they understand the concept of a geometric proof and the process of completing a geometric proof.

**Mr. Roberts:** Our U.S. History topic is the Industrial Revolution. The goal is for students to identify the economic changes that happened in our country during 1865 to 1900 and to analyze all the ways those changes impacted life in the United States.

**Ms. Bethel:** As I said, the language arts objective is about short stories. To be exact, students will know the difference between a short story and other writing methods. Also, students will demonstrate their understanding of what a short story is by writing a short story.

**Mr. Peterson:** Those objectives make sense. I really like what Ms. Matthews said about decorating her classroom to make it somehow look like the inside of the human body so students feel like they are in a body, especially in parts of the body where disease fighting happens most. Maybe all of us could decorate our rooms for the exploration unit.

**Mr. Roberts:** Good idea. Could the students do this? We have a lot of students that are very artistic. Could we use their talents to decorate the classrooms, maybe even to decorate the hallway area by our classrooms, too?

**Ms. Matthews:** What about the students who are not so artistic? What should they do while the artists are decorating the room?

**Ms. Bethel:** Oh, they could help with some part of the decorating even if they aren't super artists. Of course, we could create a variety of options so some students decorate the room to match the unit theme and the unit lessons. Decorate the room, create a skit to present information the students research, write about the unit, make a video about some part of the unit, or maybe even about all four subjects combined into one video; what else could they do?

| | |
|---|---|
| Ms. Matthews: | I get good results with the old-fashioned textbook. I don't rely on it, but I do use it. Some students never get the big ideas of science until they do the page-by-page work in the textbook. They can work toward the big concepts, but the book gets them started. |
| Mr. Peterson: | Math can be like that. Pages of math problems are no fun, but they work. At least they make students work with numbers. What really helps the most in math is when we find real-life use of the numbers. So many of the students like sports, so I make a lot of math problems for the students to do that put the math concepts into calculations about sports statistics. |
| Mr. Roberts: | That's a good idea, but it might work better with math than with other subjects. Math and sport statistics, that's a natural match. What can I connect the Industrial Revolution to that students are interested in? |
| Ms. Bethel: | Maybe baseball. I watched a great documentary on television last summer. It was all about the history of baseball. It overlaps with the years you mentioned. Maybe the telegraph and telephone from the Industrial Revolution time period could be contrasted with how people communicate now. No age-group is more fascinated with cell phones than teenagers are. |
| Mr. Roberts: | That makes sense. Now, every two weeks my students have a writing project. How should we include writing in the exploration unit? |
| Mr. Peterson: | I hope we can make it interesting. The students selected the exploration theme. Maybe before we create all of the writing assignments and other activities we could get some more input from the students. They know how they learn best. If they say "play games all day," we can't do that, of course, but the students came up with a great theme for this unit. They could probably add some good ideas for what we do day to day during this unit. |
| Ms. Bethel: | Let's do that in our classes this afternoon, and then after school today let's e-mail each other the best ideas students had. We can discuss the ideas at our team meeting tomorrow. |

**106**

CHAPTER 5

At the eighth-grade team meeting the next day, what ideas could be mentioned? The teachers' names and subjects are listed below so the reader can create the opening part of the team meeting discussion about specific ideas and activities that could be used during the exploration unit.

Mr. Roberts, social studies:

Ms. Bethel, language arts:

Ms. Matthews, science:

Mr. Peterson, math:

Now let's concentrate on ways that extreme writing could apply uniquely as part of the work done during the exploration unit in each of the four subject areas.

Social studies: In the late 1800s newspapers and magazines were very popular. Today newspapers are struggling to stay in business because of electronic Internet competition. Which do you prefer—newspapers or news websites? Interview someone who prefers the other news source. Explain the reasons that you and the other person had for preferring the news source.

Language arts: Some of you expressed a strong interest in personally exploring space. Other students said they would rather explore places on Earth. Still others prefer to explore throughout the underwater world of oceans. Write a short story of the exploration you prefer. Your story can be dramatic, fantasy, science fiction, adventure, overcoming challenges, or amusing. Include at least three characters in your short story and include at least one conflict that is resolved in your story.

Science: You had a lot of good questions for the school nurse when she came to our class to discuss how we can prevent or minimize illness. Now write the script of one episode of a television program with one of the following titles: "Ask the Doctor," "Ask the Nurse," "Medicines of the Future," "The Doctor's Office of the Future," "The Hospital of the Future," or "The Pharmacy of the Future." There are options beyond the television script format—a comic book, a radio phone-in talk show, a video game, or a website.

Math:
Many eighth-graders are interested in sports, but not all eighth-graders share that interest. To connect with knowledge, talents, and interest of all the students, the writing activity for math had to be very creative, because geometry itself can be confusing initially to students. There are many geometric theorems that apply to triangles, so that became the connection. Fashion, sports, a musical trio, architecture, home furnishing, some food shapes or servings—all of these were parts of real life where triangles were found. The students would create a theorem and write the proof. Example evaluation: left-handed batters in baseball beat out more infield grounders because the triangle of the batter, the infielder who catches the ball, and first base has a shorter side between the batter and first base than does the triangle for a right-handed batter.

The extreme writing activities for the eighth-grade subjects were not identical. The teachers did not use the identical assignment, such as write a short story about (a) the Industrial Revolution, (b) fighting illness, (c) triangles in everyday life, or (d) travel.

The teachers also let the exploration theme develop during the two weeks allocated to that unit. The students would academically explore geometry while artistically designing geometric accessories to transform the classroom into a geometric exhibition. Numbers would be calculated. Triangles, lines, line segments, angles, measurements, theorems, and proofs would be done with pencil and paper detail. The variety of teaching methods and activities would combine into an overall process that caused learning of geometry. What worked in math would not be duplicated in or forced into the other subjects.

In team meetings the teachers would trade success stories, but they would modify what worked in one class to apply that success to the uniqueness of other subjects and to the unique atmosphere of each classroom. Johnny the math student may learn geometry by connecting it to soccer, for accurately lining a field with exact soccer dimensions and precise lines requires geometry. Johnny the science student who recently had the flu could explore the topic of how the body fights illness through a study of how flu vaccinations work, not through a stretched, forced, or contrived connection with soccer.

## FOR TEACHERS ONLY: TEACHING INSIGHT 8

Some educators very sincerely state, "I could never work at a middle school. That age-group is just too unpredictable and too energetic. There's too much going on at that age for them to settle down and do the school work correctly."

Other educators very sincerely state, "I would never work anywhere except a middle school. That age-group is so curious, so lively, so open to new adventures, so dynamic. Sure, they have their moods and their moments, but they bring so much vitality to school along with enough life experience to create unlimited learning possibilities."

For teachers who work in elementary schools or in high schools, the body of knowledge about the best practice with middle school students can provide useful ideas that can be modified, as needed, to fit with elementary or high school students. If you are in the "I could never work at a middle school" group, you can still benefit from what has been learned about the best ways to educate that age-group.

## WRITING WITHIN THE HIGH SCHOOL CURRICULUM

The high school curriculum is wider in range of topics and deeper in thoroughness of study than the elementary or middle school curricula are. Extreme writing can work within the wide and deep high school curriculum with proper application. For this journey, we will follow one high school student through her classes on one day at high school.

"Hi. Sorry. No time to talk. I've got to get to the library before first-period class. The paper for English is due Monday, and I'm nowhere near started. Of course, since it's Tuesday, I have a soccer game tonight. At least the game is here, but I'll get nothing done tonight on the paper or on the test coming up." Jennifer makes great grades at school, but she has no time to waste if she is going to make great grades on everything this week.

Jennifer's friend, Ashley, can relate. "This week is so stressful. Tests and papers. It's too much, you know. I'll see you at lunch."

Jennifer and Ashley go their separate ways, Jennifer to the library and Ashley to her Physics classroom, where she has to make up a quiz she missed on Monday. She missed Monday morning classes so she could be a mentor at a middle school. Her teachers had to let her make up the work because the high school encourages participation in the mentoring program. Well, some people at the high school encourage it. Most of the high school teachers tolerate it, but many oppose it because they think classes should not be missed for anything other than unavoidable absences. The request for mentoring to be done after school got a bureaucratic rejection based on "schedule conflicts and transportation issues."

Jennifer's first block class today is Algebra II, followed by World History, Chemistry, and sophomore English to finish the four class blocks she has this week on Tuesday and Thursday. When she gets to lunch and finds Ashley, they have plenty to discuss. Jennifer begins their conversation.

Jennifer:    Sorry I had to run this morning. That English paper is taking a lot of time. We have to do this complicated character analysis or something. Why not just read the book instead of analyzing the characters? Whatever. These teachers think we have nothing to do except work full time on their class. Then we got this assignment in Algebra II class. It's actually kind of interesting, but who has the time?

Ashley:    Yeah. Time, there's just not enough. That Algebra II project was interesting. I've got that class right after you, so I guess our class had the same project. You write a conversation that the two sides of a really complex equation have with each other as they work together to solve the equation. That's different. One guy asked if he could act out the conversation, so he and another student will do that. He's pretty funny, so the skit will be cool.

Jennifer:    World History was so boring. Hey, are you going to finish those granola bars?

Ashley:    No, I'm not. I prefer the pizza slices, so the granola is all yours. What was so boring in World History? I thought you liked that class.

Jennifer:   I usually do. We had a substitute teacher today, so we had to watch some movie about some ancient war. We do have a neat project in that class. We had to pick something that we are involved in, like a school club, sport, church group, or something and tell how that activity could change world history. I chose soccer, and I'll probably make up some really wild fictional story about the U.S. winning the World Cup for women's soccer and men's soccer two times in a row and how those years led to peace with the U.S. and nations we never got along with.

Ashley:     How about this weekend? Are you going to the football game and dance Friday night?

Jennifer:   I have to work. The store has some big event Friday, so I have to be there. It's supposed to rain Friday, so I'd rather work than stand in the rain at the football game. Are you going?

Ashley:     Yeah, if my grades are up. My parents are all over my grades. College scholarships or something.

Jennifer:   That reminds me. I have to get to third-block Chemistry class early. The stuff we did yesterday made no sense to me, so she said to come early today for help before this lunch period ends. I'll see you after school.

When Jennifer and Ashley got together after school, they talked about soccer, homework, and what they had heard about some students who got suspended for 10 days each for serious abuse of the school's computer system. Jennifer and Ashley were walking home from school, so their conversation continued.

Ashley:     I heard they tried to hack into the computer system to change their grades. That's so stupid.

Jennifer:   Yeah. Now there will be some big crackdown on computer use. We'll all have some new rules to follow. This is so stupid. Wait. That gives me an idea. I need a topic for an English paper. Computer crimes. There's a topic.

Ashley:     That is so cool. You could become an expert on computer crime. Maybe the school would hire you to show them how to keep students from hacking into the system to change grades and stuff.

Jennifer:   I don't really need another job. I do need a good grade on my paper for English class, because my grade is a very high

B and I need to get it up to an A. This paper could do that. Our teacher said it could be on a topic we pick, as long as it has some controversy or conflict in it that we show both sides of. Hey, the good side of computers against the hacker side of computers. Computer nerds take on the computer criminals. This is really cool.

Ashley: Don't forget chemistry. Did that extra time help today? Oh, bad news. Right after you went to Chemistry, David came looking for you. He really wants to take you to the football game and the dance. Couldn't you leave work in time to come to the dance? You know how much he likes you.

Jennifer: Yeah, he likes me. He liked me in the fourth grade. Did he tell you that? We got in trouble in middle school writing notes to each other in the seventh grade. He got me in so much trouble last year—he called me during my third-block class when he was in his lunch period. I had left my phone on. The teacher was so mad when it rang in class! So tell me why I should go to the dance with David.

Ashley: Come on, Jennifer, any guy who has liked you since fourth grade is not the usual guy. Give him credit for liking you enough to not give up.

Jennifer: If he really liked me he would give up. I'm just not interested in going to the dance with David. I am interested in finishing my chemistry homework, eating something, and playing soccer tonight. How about you?

Ashley: I've got homework to do. Maybe I'll get it finished in time to see your soccer game. I'd like to be there. David's friend, Thomas—

Jennifer: Oh, Thomas, so that's what this is about. Tell me more.

Ashley: David's friend, Thomas, and David are going to the soccer game tonight. David likes you and, well, you know, Thomas and I sort of like each other, at least I think so.

Jennifer: Time for my homework to get done. You and Thomas have a great time at the soccer game and at the dance Friday night, but I'm not going out with David just so you can go out with Thomas.

Ashley: That's cool; well, you go get your work done and then play great tonight. I'll be watching. Maybe Thomas and I will be watching.

Students are real people living real lives right now. Jennifer and Ashley are good examples of what is real in the lives of high school students, including homework, grades, anticipation of college, school extracurricular activities, social events, dating, and many other realities. Notice that Jennifer sees some very real application of the computer crime topic to her English class assignment and to her life as a student in high school. The writing assignments for Algebra II and for World History were different, but had elements of extreme writing. The uniqueness of each high school subject can mean that the most effective learning activities in general and writing activities in particular need to precisely match the characteristics of each subject.

Writing across the curriculum will not have the maximum result if each student has the same writing task or the same type of writing task in every class day after day. Writing within the curriculum acknowledges and applies the uniqueness of each academic subject. Writing within the curriculum also acknowledges the variety of topics within each subject. The teaching activities that most effectively cause learning about the Industrial Revolution may not cause equivalent learning about the 13 colonies or the Great Depression, because each of those topics, while within U.S. History, have unique facts, impact, and participants that each connect with different life experiences of any one student.

Let's go back to Jennifer and Ashley, because their chemistry class is going to have a week of research on chemistry, careers, and modern life. What careers apply knowledge of chemistry? What parts of modern life are most impacted, perhaps made possible, by breakthroughs in consumer applications for chemistry? With those thoughts in mind, the reader is asked to create an extreme writing activity for the chemistry class as they study chemistry, careers, and modern life.

Create an extreme writing activity for chemistry:

The high school curriculum has many more subjects than the four that have been considered thus far: Algebra II, World History, Chemistry, and English. The reader is asked to now think of, or otherwise identify perhaps by going to high school websites, the total list of subjects included in the high school curriculum, including vocational/technical classes, requirements for graduation, electives, and other possibilities. Then select the subjects that most directly concern you or interest you and identify how extreme writing could be used as one of the instructional methods that cause learning in those subjects. Notice, the subjects you select are not necessarily the same subjects other readers would select. Just like students, adults also have a range of wholesome knowledge, interests, and talents.

No matter how personally, individually, meaningfully, creatively, and extremely teachers design instructional activities for students, and sometimes with students, there will be problems. Take heart—to every problem there is an equal and opposite solution. In the next chapter the increasingly complex, complicated, demanding, and exhausting realities of teaching will be confronted. The potential joys and achievements for teachers and students can help sustain determined teachers, but the increasingly difficult realities in schools must be addressed.

**6**

# WHAT CAN GO WRONG
# AND WHAT TO DO ABOUT THAT

**W**ords are to writing as notes and lyrics are to music. Notice, music has the advantage of two forces: notes and lyrics. Writing has only one force—words—or does it? Maybe there is or can be some rhythm in writing that is similar to what notes do to music.

Maybe some students never see into the rhythm, the soul, the personality, the energy, the wonder of writing. Perhaps those students see writing merely as the chore of putting enough words on enough paper to get a good enough grade to pass a class and move on. Is that attitude toward writing part of what can go wrong? Yes, but much more can go wrong. That is not pessimistic or fatalistic. That is reality, so the wise teacher anticipates the reality that something can go wrong and seeks to (1) prevent, if possible, (2) minimize and correct quickly, if only partial prevention is possible, and (3) resolve with thorough corrections if no prevention was possible.

What can go wrong? There is some temptation to say "everything," and some teaching days can be like that. The school's computer system is not working. The copy machines are broken. The unexpected fire drill interrupts your class, which was taking a test. The central office administrator who conducted a four-minute "walk-through" observation of your class recently sent a summary of what she saw that was very superficial and incomplete if contrasted with the total lesson, the planning that made the lesson possible, and the time that will be spent grading papers students wrote during the final part of class.

Some unannounced or unscheduled afternoon event will take some students out of class, and they will miss the guest speaker you announced and scheduled weeks ago. The classrooms near your room have substitute teachers again, and the noise level from those rooms limits what can be accomplished in your classroom. What's a teacher to do on days like that? What's a teacher to do when days like that stretch into weeks or months like that?

What's a teacher to do when the writing project that was assigned two weeks ago is turned in by 20 of 27 students on the due date despite a very clearly understood policy of no late work? What's a teacher to do when the writing activity done in class today got a variety of effort by students ranging from total commitment to totally ignored? What's a teacher to do when 24 out of 26 students respond enthusiastically to an extreme writing activity while the other 2 students do everything possible to disrupt class and sabotage the overall learning process? What's a teacher to do with a court-involved student who defies a judge yet is allowed back in school to defy teachers?

There is much that goes right in classrooms. Quality lessons are prepared, presented, and experienced. Students learn the basic academic skills and then build upon that foundation to graduate from high school. College scholarships are earned for superior academic achievements. Lives are touched. Second chances are provided and are reciprocated with new commitment.

Still, much more can go wrong in classrooms than people who do not work in classrooms could imagine or realize. Students arrive late and interrupt a class. Students make disruptive comments during class. Students make excuses or have their family make excuses for them—"our printer broke last night just as Jason was going to print the project for your class." Knocks on the classroom door, phone calls to the classroom, public address announcements during class all interrupt a teacher's best effort. Students verbally or physically fight. Rumors spread and tension builds in the school. A student brings a weapon, or drugs, or cell phone pornography. A student starts an Internet site that harms the reputation of an honorable teacher. Homework is not done or is only partially done.

Missed tests are not made up. The computer grading system malfunctions the day before grades must be entered in the computer for report cards. A smart, capable, conscientious student falls in with the wrong crowd and begins skipping school and failing tests.

Students continue to use cell phones during class despite being caught, having the phone taken away, and having discipline action imposed. Students come to class unprepared, with the assigned reading not done, the assigned writing not done, no pen or pencil or paper. Students whose grades make them ineligible for sports somehow get to participate. Students whose families keep taking trips during the school year expect the school to adjust to their travel schedule. Students fail a class on purpose because it will not keep them from passing for the year or graduating, or because they do not need that credit, so they disrupt or sleep or skip. Students pretend to pay attention but are really copying homework for another class during your class. Students use vulgar language directly to the face of a teacher.

Presidents, governors, state legislators, members of Congress, local officials, civic leaders, or civic misleaders make grand pronouncements about education. Could those people do the job of a classroom teacher? They would find that their speeches or sound bites about education are fantasy when contrasted with the front-line reality of working in a classroom. Some school officials at the state and/or school district level can also minimize the difficulties of classroom teaching because they never were a teacher or because it has been many years since they were a teacher. The reader is encouraged to think of additional items that his or her experience and knowledge would place on the list of what can go wrong.

So, shall we light a candle or curse the darkness, to use a phrase Eleanor Roosevelt applied in very difficult times? The candle option is much more inspiring and is much more respectable. The reality of darkness cannot be ignored, yet the power of candles cannot be denied. To illuminate the consideration of what can go wrong and what to do about that, insight and wisdom will light the way.

Capable, experienced, wise teachers were asked in May 2009 to provide insight. The emphasis of this survey was for highly skilled veteran teachers to provide guidance for first-year teachers; however, the answers given by these veterans can be useful to all educators, teachers,

administrators, and support staff—from the beginning year of a career
to the months prior to retirement. These answers can help anticipate,
prevent, or minimize what can go wrong; however, these answers remind us that although achieving educational perfection is elusive due to
so many factors out of the control of teachers, there is so much that can
be controlled or managed that ways to bring about improvements are
known, are available, and can be implemented.

The verbatim thoughts of nine very capable, respected, successful,
and experienced educators will follow. Their responses were intended
to provide specific guidance to first-year teachers or to teachers who
are very early in their career; however, each year of teaching is the first
year of every teacher's work with their current students, so the insight
can apply to all teachers. These thoughts are qualitative, so the findings are not statistically precise or based on a sufficient sample size to
project with quantitative measures. Still, these ideas can guide quality
work. These ideas can also help teachers anticipate what can go wrong
by remembering what is true about the working conditions for teachers,
what matters most in teaching, and how to replace what can go wrong
with what can be made to go right.

1. What do you know about teaching now that you wish you had
   known about teaching when you were in your first year as a
   teacher?
   a. When I first started teaching, I thought I had learned every-
      thing I needed to learn through college. Little did I know at
      that time, teaching each day in the classroom is an education
      in and of itself.
   b. I wish I had known more about the practical aspects—keeping
      records, grading, classroom management.
   c. How truly significant a difference, an impact teachers can make
      on their students.
   d. Strategies for designing meaningful, relevant activities for stu-
      dents.
   e. I wish I had known how much the profession changes each
      year. I would have liked to have known how most of my time
      would be spent dealing with things other than my students and
      my lessons.

f. I wish that better classroom management training had been around when I started teaching 23 years ago.

g. Students need to be redirected instead of yelled at.

h. I would have liked to know more about differentiated instruction and behavior strategies.

i. I did not understand how important it is to document everything.

2. What is the biggest difference between what you thought the work of teaching would be, based on what you knew before you began your career, and what you have learned about what teaching really is based on your actual career?

a. Teaching is all about the relationships you develop with your students.

b. I have been surprised by the politics that get played in schools.

c. Content can be learned. Loving students and loving teaching need to be part of who you are.

d. Not all students and not all parents/guardians have the same level of enthusiasm for learning as you do. So, relate first, then the learning will follow.

e. I thought that teaching would be mostly about my students, but instead it is about test scores.

f. College professors taught me differently than what was expected of me to do as a teacher. The two did not match at all.

g. I did not know it would involve so much emotion.

h. I was shocked during my first year to learn how many students were passed on without accountability. We have too many students who are not showing mastery of concepts.

i. The number of hats a teacher must wear is never fully understood until you are there.

3. What other words of wisdom would you like to share with people who are preparing for a teaching career or for people who are preparing to make the next year the best year of their teaching career?

a. Be organized. Have a classroom management plan. Be open to change.

b. Balance the idealism with practicality. And find a friend—someone to share ideas with, share the workload, and both keep you grounded as well as fire your enthusiasm. A colleague like that is invaluable.

c. Always remember we have entrusted to us everyone's most precious commodity—their children. Always treat your students as if they were your own. You would want the teachers of your children to do the same.

d. It's not content as much as it is kids.

e. Develop thick skin and just maintain focus on your kids. Do not let all the negative bog you down and break you—just focus on your students.

f. Continue to learn more and more about the subject you teach.

g. Treat children with two equally strong arms, one of love and one of discipline.

h. A teacher has to build a relationship with students. If they sense that you don't care, they won't care. You can't be their best friend, but you have to care about that child. We can't change the home environment, but we can change how we relate to students.

i. Persist. Press on.

Based on those insights, what can go wrong? Not being organized. Not having a thoroughly designed and implemented classroom management system. Not adjusting to the human dynamics that make each class with each group of students unique. Not developing a proper, caring, genuine teacher-student relationship. Not differentiating/individualizing instruction. Not making learning relevant to and for students. Not managing the chores and the tasks—paperwork, meetings, documentation. Not recharging and not nourishing your own emotions, energy, and frame of mind. Not advancing your knowledge of teaching and of your subject matter. Letting anything get in the way of students and their education being the top priorities.

The reminders in this chapter about what can go wrong with classroom work in general and about what teachers need to remember or to do are very useful thoughts for overall application by teachers. Applying these thoughts directly to teaching students with writing activities is the next topic.

What can go wrong in the process of teaching students through writing activities? For the purpose of answering this question, the assumption is that students are literate, have done enough writing to function in the basic mechanics of writing, and have completed some variety of writing work at school. Our purpose here is not to seek ways to make students literate. Other books and other resources address basic writing skill development—although some of those skills, such as spelling, may require a lifetime to master.

Our purpose here is to maximize the learning in any subject at any grade level by the most effective, selective, productive use of writing as one of the many available teaching resources. So what can go wrong when a teacher uses a writing activity to cause learning? The list below is a beginning, but the reader is asked to add to the list.

1. The student just refuses to do the work.
2. The topic of the activity is very confusing.
3. The topic of the activity gets a response of "When are we ever going to use this?" or "When are we ever going to need to know this in real life?"
4. The assignment is just not designed well or organized so students clearly understand what they are to do, how they are to do this work, and why.
5. The assignment is generic.
6. The assignment is being given to students because the teacher is required to use a writing activity each week, not because the assignment is the best way to teach these students today.
7. The teacher is not at all interested in the assignment.
8. There is nothing in the assignment that connects with the knowledge, interests, or talents of students.
9. It will be easy for students to cheat by using Internet material as their own or by getting another student to do their work for them.
10. The activity appears to be overwhelming, even for capable, conscientious students.
11. There are some writing errors in the handout that told students about the writing project.

12. Spelling errors are increasing for many students.
13.
14.
15.

The list of what can go wrong will increase as the due date nears and then when the due date arrives. "I lost my sheet about the assignment. Can I get another one?" "Oh, that's due tomorrow. I better get started." "I can pass even if I don't do that assignment." "Well, about that assignment. I just could not get my computer to print it." "I forgot." "I've been so busy." "I really did not understand that assignment."

To every problem there is an equal and opposite solution. Now that what can go wrong has been identified, the topic becomes what to do about that. For each item in the prior list of what can go wrong, a possible action or actions will be provided. Room is included for the reader to list an additional solution or solutions.

1. The student just refuses to do the work.
   a. Repeat the instruction. Use words such as "the instruction I am giving you is to do this assignment" as you point to the assignment or as you provide another copy.
   b. Document that the student was given a clear, personal instruction to do the work. This strengthens the case for discipline action if that action becomes necessary.
   c. Check on the student soon to see if any work has been done and document the results or lack of results. Pay equal attention to each student—the students who are working deserve your time and the student who is not working may be amused with dominating your time and attention.
   d.
   e.
2. The topic of the activity is very confusing.
   a. Ask a student to read your rough-draft version of the assignment to see if it makes sense. Make improvements.
   b. Ask another teacher to read your rough-draft version of the assignment to see if it makes sense. Make improvements.

   c. Contrast the wording of and structure of this assignment with prior assignments that were fully understood by students.

   d.

   e.

3. The topic of the activity gets a response of "When are we ever going to use this?" or "When are we ever going to need to know this in real life?"

   a. "Great questions. You'll notice that all of the choices you have for this writing project come from the list of career interests everyone told me about. So as soon as you begin your career is one answer to your question. Today this assignment helps you prepare for that career."

   b. Realize that some complaints are unfounded. Some students like to complain. Some students complain in hope of getting the assignment reduced or delayed.

   c. Let another student answer the question. "Well, we discussed connections like that yesterday, so I included your ideas when I designed this project. Who remembers what we discussed yesterday and can give us a summary of that?"

   d.

   e.

4. The assignment is just not designed well or organized so students clearly understand what they are to do, how they are to do this work, and why.

   a. This should be obvious to the teacher as the assignment is being designed and written. Write the assignment and then reread it later to see if it still makes sense or not.

   b. Revise the assignment with the students. Take their questions and input to clarify, strengthen, and improve the assignment itself and the students' understanding of the assignment.

   c. Make this an exercise in the importance of revisions to writing. Have the students discuss the assignment as a class as you lead the discussion. Then everyone rewrites the assignment. Combine the student versions with your version to create the best revised version. Keep the objective of the activity intact, or strengthen it, but revise the explanation and related details.

    d.

    e.

5. The assignment is generic.

    a. Do not use prepackaged, prefabricated assignments that come in the boxes of supplementary materials that accompany textbooks.

    b. Do not use last year's or last decade's assignments, even if the results were good when those activities were originally used. Your current students are not identical to your prior students.

    c. Make the assignment extreme, meaning make it connect with the wholesome knowledge, interests, and talents of students.

    d.

    e.

6. The assignment is being given to students because the teacher is required to use a writing activity each week.

    a. If the weekly writing activity requirement is official school policy, comply. There is no need for or excuse for insubordination. Do offer ideas for improving the policy and get involved in the proper process of revising the policy. Make each required activity meaningful and purposeful.

    b. Until the policy is changed, make the most of it. You and your colleagues can trade ideas so every teacher knows what type of writing activities are getting good results.

    c. Accept the reality that this is the current policy. Do not curse the darkness of the policy. Light a candle to get the most good out of the policy. Create extreme writing activities for your students to do weekly. That may be more often than you prefer or than you need, but you can make it productive and efficient. Vary the length and objective of the weekly assignments.

    d.

    e.

7. The teacher is not at all interested in the assignment.

    a. One of the four factors of great teachers is that they are enthusiastic about students, learning, and teaching. You chose the career of teaching. You chose the subjects and the grade levels you are certified to teach. You have been enthusiastic and interested before, so you can be again.

    b. Teaching is increasingly difficult, demanding, and exhausting work. It is essential to take great care of your heart, mind, body, and soul. It is easier to be enthusiastic when you are healthy and at peace.

    c. Your students deserve the best educational experiences possible, including fascinating writing activities that their teacher is excited about.

    d.

    e.

8. There is nothing in the assignment that connects with the knowledge, interests, or talents of students.

    a. Why not? All knowledge is connected, according to the liberal arts concept of learning. Look again, find connections, include connections.

    b. Have the students think of and add the connections.

    c. Format your lessons so a connection is always included in the fundamental lesson plan design. Think of connections as required rather than as optional. We know that connections work, so put them to work for you and your students.

    d.

    e.

9. It will be easy for students to cheat by using Internet material as their own or by getting another student to do their work for them.

    a. To the extent that writing assignments are individualized and personalized—as extreme writing helps assignments become—what each student writes is increasingly unique and decreasingly Internet "cut-and-paste" ordinary.

    b. Computer resources can help teachers check what students turn in against material that is on the Internet.

    c. Listen. Students talk. Work with your colleagues. If all teachers listen carefully, someone may hear what a student says about cheating. Ask school administrators and parents/guardians of alleged cheaters to help resolve suspected cheating.

    d.

    e.

10. The activity appears to be overwhelming, even for capable, conscientious students.

a. Great teachers challenge their students. Great teachers do not impose the impossible on students. What may seem overwhelming to students at first, may actually be a very useful challenge.

b. Perhaps an adjustment is necessary. "People support what they help create." If the due date is extended a few days, that may be ample. You and the students agree on the revised due date. There is much shared responsibility, shared commitment, and shared power in the new statement, "The due date we agreed on is next Tuesday, December 10, instead of this Friday, December 6."

c. Students need to learn time management and work management. Show the students how to divide the large projects into many small parts that can be done in segments of 15 minutes, 30 minutes, 1 hour. Then have each student write a schedule beginning with today and going through the minute the project is due. They create a time/work management plan.

d.

e.

11. There are some writing errors in the handout that told students about the writing project.

a. Proofread. Proofread more. Keep proofreading.

b. Give students class participation points when they find an error in any material you give them.

c. Be glad they found the error. Acknowledge their alert reading. Make the corrections. Proofread better.

d.

e.

12. Spelling errors are increasing for many students.

a. Keep a list of the words students misspell and have a weekly spelling test.

b. Spelling counts, so count spelling as part of the grade for each writing assignment.

c. Have an occasional spelling bee.

d.

e.

13.

a.

b.

c.

14.
   a.
   b.
   c.
15.
   a.
   b.
   c.

The writing assignment has been turned in. The teacher grades the writing assignment. The results are varied. A few great writings, some good writings, some average, and a very few that were unacceptable. Now what? How does the teacher give great writers the opportunity to build upon their skills, give good or average writers the opportunity to acquire more skills, and the very weak writers the experiences needed to gain basic skills? Consider the following approach.

Time for plan B and, perhaps, plan C will also be needed. In fact, each writing activity can include an automatic plan B designed as follows:

   a. If you made a grade of A on the writing assignment, you write an explanation of what was done so well that you earned an A. You also write at least one specific improvement that could be made in your paper.
   b. If you made a grade of B on the writing assignment, you write an explanation of what was good about the paper. You also write at least three specific improvements that could be made in your paper.
   c. If you made a grade of C on the writing assignment, you write an explanation of what needed to be done better. You also write at least five specific improvements that could be made in your paper.
   d. If you made a grade of D on the writing assignment, you write an explanation of what needed to be done better. You also write at least seven specific improvements that could be made in your paper. You must rewrite the paper, make the seven improvements you indicated, and turn in both the original and the revised paper in two days.
   e. If you turned in a paper, you write a detailed description of why the grade was F. You precisely match the assignment details

against what you turned in to specify everything that was not done or that was not done well. You will list at least 10 improvements than can be made in your paper. You must rewrite the paper, make the 10 improvements you indicated, and turn in both the original and the revised paper in two days.

f. If you did not turn in the assignment, you will write an explanation of what the assignment was, of why you did not do the assignment, and of what you could have done and should have done so you would have completed the assignment correctly and on time. You will turn in the original assignment and the explanation, both done completely and correctly, in one day. Your parent or guardian will call the teacher today or tomorrow so they are aware of this situation. Whether any credit is given will depend on the policy of the teacher and/or of the school.

What would be included in plan C? Let's create a list. Space is provided for your ideas.

a. The student has to come to school early or stay late to do the assignment correctly and completely.
b. The student meets with his or her school counselor.
c. If the student did not comply with plan B, discipline action for defiance could be considered.
d. The parent/guardian meets at school with the teacher and the student.
e. The student's grade on the assignment is reduced if plan B was not done completely, correctly, and on time. If the grade had been an F, class participation points could be lost or a second F could be entered in the grade book.
f.
g.
h.
i.
j.

In the extreme writing process much can and, if implemented effectively, will go right. In the human process of education, meaning of causing learning, perfection has not been attained. On a given day at most schools, much great or good work is done; however, some average, poor, or failing work is done, and some work is avoided. On a given day at most schools, much great or good behavior is shown by students; however, some defiant, disruptive, unacceptable, or worse misbehavior may occur. The earlier cited words of insight and wisdom from highly skilled, experienced teachers can provide guidance to help show teachers how to maximize good experiences and how to minimize what can go wrong.

Part of getting any writing process, including extreme writing, to go right is to do the work of revising and revising written material. The next chapter is about the reality that writing is not at its best until it has been revised and revised.

## FOR PRINCIPALS ONLY: ADMINISTRATOR INSIGHT 6

When a principal notices that everything that could go wrong for a teacher is going wrong, despite all effort made by that teacher, action is needed. Ideally, the school administrators are sufficiently aware of such situations to offer interventions, ideas, help, and encouragement before the problems increase so much that the conscientious teacher who has done all she knows to do decides to quit.

When a principal knows that a few students in one class are causing repeated problems for a teacher, take early action. Go to that classroom during that class daily. See the teacher before or after school. Check with other teachers about those students. Involve the families of each student. Impose discipline action.

Some students will not respond to the discipline options a teacher has. Principals can take additional discipline actions. The presence of a school administrator in a classroom day after day may solve the problem, or punishments only administrators can impose may help, so do what works best for everyone involved.

## FOR TEACHERS ONLY: TEACHING INSIGHT 9

What goes right at school usually far surpasses in quantity the number of actions that go wrong. Give yourself credit for the many successes of each day.

When something goes wrong, it can linger on your mind for hours, days, or longer. That is destructive. Do everything you can to cause learning in your classroom. Document your efforts. Keep school administrators informed of the successes and of the difficulties. Show that you have taken every possible step to get a defiant student to learn. At that point insist that the principal, a school counselor, the student's family, and other available people at school or in the school district get involved.

Schools are dealing with some increasingly troubled students for whom much more is needed than a varied instructional approach. Require of yourself that you do everything a teacher can do to help each student. At that point you have done your best, and other people must do their part.

## 7

# IT IS NOT THE BEST WRITING UNTIL IT HAS BEEN REVISED

The words "If I had that to do over again" are usually followed by a description of an action, a statement, a decision that would have been done differently if that were possible. Given some reflection, some analysis, some unfortunate results, some better thinking, and the elusive second chance to do something over tells us that we could have done better. Because time cannot go backward, we cannot undo what we did, so a lesson is learned and we promise to do better next time.

When writing is revised, the writer gets to do the writing over again. Perhaps the passage of time has brought a new insight. Perhaps reading the words tells the writer that what was thought has not been expressed yet in words that accurately or fully convey the thought. Perhaps there are newly noticed errors of spelling, punctuation, or sentence structure. Reaction from a reader or comments from a teacher can guide revisions.

Revision is to writing as remodeling or renovation is to a building. A remodeled house that gets painted, that gets new carpet, that gets new windows, and that gets new landscaping is still the same structure—foundation, walls, roof—but certainly has an improved appearance and will be much more pleasant to live in as a residence.

The owner of the house is pleased that the appearance of the home has improved through the remodeling, and it just seems more comfortable to live in, but something else is needed. While the remodeling was being done, some water damage from a roof leak was noticed. Then a cracked wall in the basement indicated problems with years of settling that actually compromised the foundation of the house. The roof was replaced, the water damage was repaired, and new support was added to reinforce the basement walls and the foundation. These renovations actually impacted and revised the structure of the house.

When writing is revised, some of the original wording, thinking, and organization will remain. Some changes will be made to strengthen the impact of what is written, to be more clear, to more accurately communicate the intended meaning, and to simply "sound" or read better. Some of these revisions may be as simple as remodeling or as complex as renovation. Whether the original version was awful, ordinary, or excellent, revision of writing is a proper pursuit of that which is better, that which is higher quality, that which completely communicates the best possible idea in the best possible way.

There are some parts of life in which students expect revision, actually welcome revision. The football team that is losing 21–7 at halftime makes some revisions to its original game plan. The car wash that was going to help the cheerleaders raise money gets rained out, so the schedule has to be changed. Bad weather causes school to be closed, which means a school day has to be added to the school year in May or June. High school graduation requirements are increased, so additional classes must be taken, forcing schedule changes for the high school years. The store where a 17-year-old works part time had two people quit yesterday, so his or her work schedule was revised to the maximum hours allowed for a high school student. Fashions and fads change, so people revise what they wear, what music they listen to, what phrases they use in conversation, and what entertainment is most appealing.

An elementary school student, Mary, may be told one Saturday morning by her parent that she must clean up her room that morning. Mary proudly tells her mother very soon that the room is clean. Mom's inspection of the room finds that much more work is needed. *Clean* to Mary meant that Mary could easily find everything, whether it was on the floor, in a closet, on a piece of furniture, on the bed, or just thrown somewhere behind something. Mom understood *clean* to be all items neatly put in the proper place, nothing on the floor, all clothes hung up carefully in the closet, and no clutter anywhere.

Mary and Mom had to revise their mutual understanding of the term *clean your room*, so they made a checklist. The requirements of a clean room were on the checklist. Every Saturday morning, Mary would clean her room. She had to keep cleaning it until her efforts matched the checklist and the inspection by her mother. Some Saturday mornings, Mary had very little to revise after her first effort to clean the room. Some other Saturday mornings required multiple revisions. The checklist removed any need for debate or interpretation. The room would be cleaned and cleaned again until it was in superior condition according to the checklist requirements and according to inspection by Mary's mother.

Paula is a very conscientious eighth-grade student. She always makes the honor roll. She is active in Girl Scouts and in the youth group at her church. She started a new club at her school, Grant Middle School: Grant Recycles Energy for the Environment Now (GREEN). She decided to get involved in the musical her school would present. She got one of the leading parts. Rehearsals began in March for the performances, which would be in mid-May.

Being in the musical was exciting, enjoyable, demanding, and sometimes confusing. "The director keeps trying one thing and then another. We walk through a scene one way and then we walk through it another way. We sing a song one way and then we add some dancing, but then we change the dancing."

When the performances were completed in May, Paula thought back to those March and April rehearsals. As people congratulated Paula, the other cast members, and the stage managers, Paula said to one friend, "If they only knew. The show they just saw is nothing like it was when we began. Everything changed." The result of those revisions was a series of superior performances in May.

The high school marching band begins work in June, continues through July, and when school starts in August, members take band as a class and have another rehearsal daily after school. The performances at halftime of football games and at competitions lead to the state marching band tournament in late October. From the first note and the first step in June through the final note and the final step in October, practice, rehearsal, and revisions are followed by more practice, rehearsal, and revisions. It is understood by everyone involved in the marching band that reaching the goal of winning competitions and of being a state champion can come only through more and better practice, rehearsal, and revisions.

For some students who accept the importance of revisions when applied to cleaning their room, rehearsing for a school musical, or practicing with the marching band, or to any other good part of their life that is properly enhanced through revisions, the importance of revision can be rejected when applied to school writing assignments, activities, or projects. Other students may comply with the requirement to revise their writing because they always follow the teacher's instructions, because they are concerned about their grade, or because they would like to stay out of trouble. Some students eagerly participate in revising their writing because they have set a high standard for themselves, which accepts nothing less than the best they can do, the best they can be, and the best they can become.

"We're losing. We're losing 21–7. Is the other team two touchdowns better than we are? No. They aren't any better than we are. But in the first half of this game they played better than we did. How many blocks did we miss? Two touchdowns' worth. How many tackles did we miss? Two touchdowns' worth. It is true, they figured out how to stop our short passes. Okay. In the second half we block better, we tackle better, we run the ball more, and when we pass the ball, it will usually be for long distance. And if all of that does not work, we'll change the lineup until we find the right group of football players who can get the job done tonight."

Contrast that statement from a high school football coach speaking to his team in the locker room during halftime of a game with the following statement from a high school English teacher speaking to her first-period class in the classroom moments after returning to each student the rough draft of a paper in which each student had written an alternative ending for a novel the class had read recently.

"We're losing our creative edge. We're losing the vibrant, energetic creativity that had been your strength in the first semester. I know you are beginning to anticipate graduation from high school, but that is three months away. Your first-semester papers were generally better than these papers I just graded. In fact, you will notice that I attached a copy of your best paper from the first semester to your current paper. For every one of you, the grade was better, the ideas were better, the writing was better on the old paper I attached."

The teacher pauses to let silence inspire thinking, feelings, and some useful uncertainty within each student. "Months ago you figured out how to write with purpose, creativity, insight, bold ideas, precise word choices, accurate spelling, and correct punctuation. As you rewrite the alternative-ending paper, get all of those fundamentals back to the previous level of high quality. Also, create a new alternative ending that will force you to rethink this paper. Create the alternative ending that best applies the skills you have but did not fully use. Now, we'll use this class period for you to begin rewriting. As you do that, I will walk around and talk individually with you to be sure you understand my comments on your paper and to see what you plan to do differently. So read your paper, read my comments, think, we will talk, and you will do magnificent writing."

What response would the football team members have toward the comments from their coach? Would they disagree and say that losing 21–7 was good enough? Would they refuse to implement some changes in the second half? Would they reject a revised game plan for the second half that was based on the actual results from the first half? Would they fully accept, fully support, and fully implement the instructions from the coach?

What response would the high school seniors have toward the comments from their English teacher? Would they disagree and say that their declining work quality was still earning a passing grade, which was good enough? Would they refuse to implement changes to their rough draft? Would they reject a revised plan for the next section of the assignment? Would they fully accept, fully support, and fully implement the instructions from the teacher?

Many variables will collectively determine the answers to those questions about how the football team responds to the coach and about how the senior English class responds to the teacher. It is easy to stereotypically assume that the football players dedicate themselves 100 percent to the second-half plan, although the coach did indicate that in the first half the total dedication to blocking and tackling was missing. It is also easy to assume that some or many of the seniors would silently or verbally protest the additional English class task given to them; however, it is possible that the teacher and the students in the English classroom have a mutual commitment that is the foundation for acceptance of an honest evaluation.

"Don't tell me I did great work if I did not do great work. I want to be ready for college, really ready. Make me do my best work even if I complain. I need you to never let me get by with less than my best." The high school senior may not make that statement in those words to the English teacher, but the high school seniors have communicated that standard. The students also know that their teacher has set that standard for herself and for her students from the first day of school.

Revising written work to make each piece of writing the very best possible is no surprise to anyone in this senior English extreme writing classroom where the writing approach is as extreme as are the standards. No person expects a football coach to seek less than the best possible result from his team. Extreme writing teachers have the same requirement for their students as coaches have for their athletes.

Please continue to think of what academic instruction of extreme writing could learn from athletic training and coaching. A high school football team, depending upon the state's athletic rules, may be allowed to begin practice in mid-July for a football season that begins in late August and continues into November. For the five or six weeks during July and August, as practice follows practice, there might be a scrimmage or two, but almost all of the July and August time is spent on drill and practice, running plays over and over, more drills to work on one particular part of a skill, more practice to prepare for any possible game situation, group instruction so athletes who play a particular position learn the details of that position while other athletes work on the skills they need for their position, more drills or more repetition of the same drill, and an occasional comment from a coach that "we will keep doing this over and over until everyone gets it right."

That is the athletic version of revision. It works in sports, in school play rehearsals, in quick-recall academic team practices, in marching band practices, in speech and debate preparation for competitions, and in many other extracurricular activities where the pursuit of perfection is based upon repetitive practice of skills and measured improvement of skills.

Writing is a similar skill in that it responds to repetitive practice to improve ability. Writing also is similar to sports in that athletic skills can be divided into step-by-step sub-skills that collectively become the desired comprehensive ability. What a football team does in an actual game was practiced not as a simulated game, but as a series of many drills to develop the multiple skills that are then combined into one play, which is also practiced repetitively. The skills of writing can be itemized and practiced separately with the eventual goal of combining those separate skills into the overall ability to write well.

Ideas, words, sentences, paragraphs, pages are the steps toward a complete school writing assignment. The pages of writing will be only as good as the paragraphs. The paragraphs will be only as good as the sentences. The sentences will be only as good as the words. The words will be only as good as the ideas to which the words give expression, form, structure, and life.

The ideas will be only as good as the assignment that inspires, ignites, provokes, and energizes the vibrant thinking that creates lively ideas, which take shape through carefully chosen words that become part of expressive sentences, powerful paragraphs, and high-quality writing overall. Extreme writing helps especially to provide the first step in that process—a topic put into assignment form that intrigues the student so the thinking process is profound and the subsequent writing is potent, meaningful, worthwhile, personally important, and academically productive.

The best writing emerges from a process of revision and more revision. The requirement for the best writing is revise, revise more, and keep revising. "But I already rewrote it once. That's enough, isn't it? Can't I just do something else?" Contrast the following comment: "Yeah, that's true. I'm thinking of the job I really want, but I could explain my reasons better. I could put more of me into the paper so the reader knows why, you know, this is the job I really want. I mean, if this letter really was my job application, it would have to be more convincing. I get it. Put more of me in it. Make it read as well as I sound when I talk about my dream job."

The difference in those two reactions to rewriting a school writing assignment is in the extent to which the student was, to be blunt, selfishly benefiting from the assignment. It takes more than the fear of the worst possible grade to evoke the best possible thinking, writing, and commitment from students. Extreme writing helps create personal

commitment from each student by making the writing personally meaningful to each student. When the work is personally meaningful, more
crudely expressed as selfishly relevant, the commitment to writing and
to rewriting is more likely to be sufficiently strong to result in high-
quality achievement.

The first step in revising is in revision of thinking. What? You read
correctly; before writing can be improved through revisions, the thinking that preceded the writing must be examined, reviewed, and revised.
The first revision of thinking is done by the extreme writing teacher
before the writing assignment is given to the students.

## CASE STUDY 6

School policy requires a ninth-grade teacher to use a writing assignment for a grade at least once per week. This is to be separate from
any test, quiz, or other graded work. The school is in a school district
in a state where the state department of education issued regulations
that students in all grades and in all classes would have additional writing "Tasks, Requirements, Activities, Standards, and Help." When the
regulation was proclaimed, many teachers were amused at the acronym,
TRASH, which apparently the regulation creators had not noticed.
When informed of the acronym, they quickly modified the regulation
to "Tasks, Requirements, Activities, Instruction, and Networking." The
networking was included to encourage use of technology, whether that
helped with writing or not, because the national trend was that anything
related to technology must be good.

The new acronym, TRAIN, was unfortunate for two reasons: (1) the
regulation seemed to be railroaded—approved quickly with very little
consideration of alternatives—and (2) the goal of training is to make everyone perform identically, which, in the reality of classrooms, overlooks
the human variable and the human real world.

What would have happened if teachers were given a writing assignment about the new writing regulation? Ms. Kim Finney, the ninth-
grade Civics teacher, knew what her response would be. "Bureaucracies cannot teach. Bureaucracies can reorganize, reform, and regulate,
so they do that often. Reorganizing, reforming, and regulating cannot

teach; therefore, each new reorganization, new reform, and new regulation is followed by another new reorganization, new reform, and new regulation in a search for the elusive reorganization, reform, and regulation trio that actually improves student achievement. Student achievement happens in classrooms, not in or through bureaucracies."

Ms. Finney is fond of saying that "high school is the only real world." She does not separate school from real life, because her perception is that life at school is as real as life can get and that the high school years are uniquely real. The opportunities, challenges, personal changes, decisions, experiences, temptations, potential for achievement, friendships made, mistakes made, mistakes corrected, mistakes prevented, lessons learned, career foundations built, inches grown, maturity gained, and experiences shared during the years between 14 years old and 18 years old, from entering ninth grade to graduating from high school, are absolutely real. Ms. Finney thrives on sharing these real years with her very real ninth-graders.

The discussions in her classroom on Monday, Tuesday, and Wednesday were scholarly and creative, productive and Socratic, all by design yet also with time given to unexpected learning moments, which the classroom community of a teacher and her students mutually committed to each other and to learning could produce. The students usually responded to Ms. Finney's unlimited devotion to them with extra shared trust and mutual dedication.

After school on Wednesday Ms. Finney thought that with two days left in the week she had to quickly create and complete the weekly writing activity. Of course, she had already prepared a writing topic and task as part of her lesson planning, but the discussions this week had already surpassed that original writing topic. The students had been intrigued with Supreme Court cases relating to the Bill of Rights, and Ms. Finney sought a real writing activity that built upon those discussions of Supreme Court cases and that related to the real life of high school students.

"Pick one of the provisions in the Bill of Rights and explain how it applies to a high school situation." No, Kim Finney could do better than that, and she knew her students deserved better. She revised her first draft.

"Pick one of the guaranteed freedoms or rights protected by the Bill of Rights and apply that to a rule at school to see if the rule is consistent with the Bill of Rights." Better. Ms. Finney's students had read, discussed, and analyzed the Student Rights and Responsibilities book. They had read, discussed, and analyzed the Bill of Rights. A lot of the classroom discussion related to the first amendment to the U.S. Constitution. The students had been very fascinated with Supreme Court cases related to the First Amendment. With that in mind, Ms. Finney revised her second draft. A few more minutes of the teacher revising the writing topic would result in much better work by her students.

"The following new rules could be considered by our school to deal with various problems. The concerns or problems these potential rules address have been discussed by the faculty. Evaluate these proposals to determine if they are consistent with the First Amendment to the U.S. Constitution.

1. To prevent hallway traffic congestion, students may gather in the halls in groups of four or fewer during time before first period or during time between class periods.
2. To improve the quality of life for everyone at school, vulgar language from anyone at any time is not allowed.
3. To improve the overall character of the school, public displays of affection are not allowed.
4. Expression of opinions about political or religious topics will not include wearing clothing, jewelry, symbols, or other materials that could be disruptive of a proper educational climate."

Ms. Finney could anticipate the great thinking and sincere writing of ideas, opinions, and reasoning her students would do on Thursday. The Bill of Rights, especially the First Amendment to the U.S. Constitution, would relate directly to the real lives of ninth-grade students at their high school.

When her students came to first-period Civics class on Thursday, they were given a copy of the writing topic and task immediately after the bell rang to begin class. When Jason raised his hand and asked, "Are those serious? There's no way we can be told to just have four people in a group. What if more people show up to talk? How can we make them leave?" Jason seemed to speak for everyone, as several hands went up.

Ms. Finney decided to let those four students speak as a way to warm up everyone's thinking. Then she instructed the students to begin thinking and writing on their own in rough-draft form, which means ideas, phrases, outlines, and thoughts. The sentences and paragraphs would follow, but first there was thinking and prewriting. Ms. Finney walked throughout the classroom to be sure that all students were working on this writing activity, to answer questions, and to acknowledge good work.

Within about seven or eight minutes, all of the students had compiled some prewriting thoughts that applied the First Amendment to the four possible new rules at school. Ms. Finney had seen the work done by each student. A few students had needed guidance to fully understand the assignment. Some other students had questions about the First Amendment or about Supreme Court cases they had read for class and how those cases might apply to these new rules.

Ms. Finney closely watched two students who sat and did nothing for two more minutes. She spoke to one of those students, who said he was thinking. In no time he was writing good thoughts, so he must have needed the extra think time. The other student who was doing no writing apparently intended to do no writing at all. Ms. Finney knew the student loved skateboarding and often visited with his skateboarding friends before school in a large group. Ms. Finney asked him how the possible rule about groups of four would apply to him. He had no comment, which was out of character for him. Ms. Finney encouraged him to keep thinking and to start writing, but she gave him another minute or two as she walked throughout the room.

She checked on Zeke again, and still there was no writing. "Zeke, you need to begin writing. Which of the new rules would you prefer to write about first? I thought that group of four rule would interest you." Zeke replied, "These rules are dumb." Now Ms. Finney had something to work with. "Zeke, write down exactly what you just said. Then use words from the First Amendment to prove that the rules are dumb. You are off to a good start." Zeke did not think his "these rules are dumb" comment was a good start or a good anything. Ms. Finney is a master of using student input as a learning resource. Zeke's thinking and writing soon were of better quality and of more quantity than he had expected.

The thinking and prewriting served as the foundation for the first draft. Ms. Finney led a short discussion about the four rules and the First Amendment. Based on the work she had seen every student do and on the ideas she heard expressed, she was confident that the class individually and collectively could write the first draft well.

"Good work. Now, take the thoughts you wrote and create one paragraph for each of the four new rules. If you prefer, you may write two paragraphs about one rule, and a single paragraph about two other rules. That way you could emphasize one rule that most interested you. Let's take the next 10 minutes or so and see if you can complete your first draft of these four paragraphs."

Ms. Finney stretched the 10 minutes into 13 minutes because the time was being used productively, students were seriously working, and because everyone was finished at the end of 13 minutes. The students who finished earlier knew without having to be told today—it was standard operating procedure in Ms. Finney's classroom—that you used the remaining time to read what you had written and to begin improving, editing, and changing what you had written.

The papers were turned in, and the next activity began. "You are getting a copy of the Supreme Court case of Tinker v. Des Moines. It deals with high school students who, a few decades ago, got in trouble at school for wearing armbands. Read the Supreme Court decision on your own silently, and then we'll discuss it."

As the students read, Ms. Finney glanced at each paper that had been turned in. She was not grading the papers—that would take a lot of time and total concentration tonight at home. She was confirming that every student had completed the assignment. She found two papers that needed more work, so she told those students what needed to be done right now. They completed the work and then got back to the reading. The discussion about the Supreme Court case was as vigorous as oral arguments before the Supreme Court. Class ended with a reminder that on Friday a local lawyer would visit the class to answer questions about laws, the courts, and the Constitution.

In the final minute of class Ms. Finney asked if there were additional questions for the lawyer. The students had written questions on Monday, and those questions were e-mailed to the lawyer on Tuesday. One student asked to see what the lawyer thought of the Tinker v. Des

Moines case. Ms. Finney promised to e-mail that question to the lawyer during lunch. The bell rang, and the students walked out into the hallway noticing that there were some groups of five or more students gathered at various places. What would the new rule say, and what would the Constitution say about such groups?

Ms. Finney always gets papers, tests, and quizzes back to students within two days of when the work was turned in. The first drafts were returned on Monday. Each paper had comments written by Ms. Finney. The comments were directly related to what each student wrote and provided clear direction about how to revise the paper, without doing the revision work for the students. Ms. Finney's comments were designed to guide each student to see their writing anew, to think about their ideas and the written expression of those ideas anew. Ms. Finney's comments were just enough direction to guide the students, but not to do the work for any student.

Monday morning's class began with the papers being returned. There was a grade on each paper along with the individualized comments. Each step of the writing process earns a grade. The first part of class on this Monday was set aside for students to thoroughly read their papers, to thoroughly read and then think about Ms. Finney's comments, and then to list specific changes that needed to be made in the paper.

Commonly it was expected that the number of needed changes varied from student to student, but the minimum number was known to be five; the usual number was more than five but was never so overwhelming as to appear impossible. Ms. Finney knows that she will work with her ninth-graders for an entire school year. Much progress would be made through a continuous sequence of small yet essential steps. This Monday was one more important step in that journey of a year.

The second draft of this paper about the First Amendment was evaluated and graded against this standard—what changes were made, how these changes improved the paper, and what changes were still needed.

With every student involved in reading his or her paper and Ms. Finney's comments, the thoughts turn to rewriting the paper. The revised paper is due on Tuesday. The fast pace is to build upon the high level of interest and awareness that the topic has created in the past week. Some time is given in class on Monday for students to begin revising their papers. Ms. Finney circulates throughout the classroom to interact with each student or to acknowledge the work each student is doing. Because the students are very productive, Ms. Finney extends the time in class for working on revisions to about one-half of the total class time.

The second half of class takes the students to the years 1788 to 1791. The students learn that what became the Bill of Rights was not exactly what was proposed. Some other amendments were considered, but were not added to the Constitution. The students learn the history and the political science aspects of the process of the Bill of Rights getting added to the U.S. Constitution. They also learn that Amendments One to Ten, as they are known now, resulted from some rewriting and some revision.

On Tuesday the students in Ms. Finney's first-period Civics class and in her two other Civics classes turn in their revised papers. Ms. Finney also teaches two U.S. History classes. Her five classes are divided into morning and afternoon portions, which she requested. Civics classes are periods one, two, and three. U.S. History classes are fourth and sixth periods, with a planning period schedule for fifth period.

With three classes turning in rewritten papers on Tuesday, Ms. Finney has much grading to do because of her standard for returning the papers within one or two days. In this case, the first-period papers are returned on Wednesday and the papers for the other Civics classes are returned on Thursday. What happens when these second-draft revisions are returned?

For some students the assignment is completed with the second draft because those students have surpassed all requirements. Please note, meeting the requirements is not sufficient; rather, success is defined as surpassing the requirements for the extreme writing activity.

For students who have met the requirements after completing the second draft, there is more work to be done. Ms. Finney has explained to the students that repeatedly meeting the requirements means that you have reached and stayed at a plateau. The goal is to always improve, so the standards and the requirements have to be continually surpassed. Every month or so, Ms. Finney increases the standards and the requirement, so students have to surpass the old standard, but soon what used to be a quality of work that surpassed the old standard simply meets the new standard.

For the students who have not met the requirements after completing the second draft, there is much more work to be done. These students and the students who met but did not surpass the requirement have been given comments and instruction from Ms. Finney on their second draft. The third draft is due in two days, but it is not called the third draft. It is called the perfected revision.

This revision begins with the student making a list of everything in the graded second draft that is imperfect. The second draft, the list of imperfections, and the perfected revision will need to be turned in two days after the second draft has been returned to the students. The students always rise to the occasion.

The perfected revision is always the best work in the prewrite, first draft, second draft, and perfected revision process. This does not frustrate Ms. Finney. She does not chastise students with questions such as "Why didn't you do great work like that at the start?" because she knows that there is a process in, a sequence for, and a human element to high-quality work. Her goal is for each student to write very well, not for each student to write very well instantly. She realizes that instant writing is never the best writing. It's not the best writing until it has been revised and revised.

Notice, no class time is provided for students to work on their perfected revision. Students who seek Ms. Finney's help on the perfected revision will easily find her available before school or after school, but the student must make that effort and take that initiative. Ms. Finney is using extreme writing to teach writing. She is using the revision process to teach responsibility and persistence, in addition to teaching students how to write at an impressive level. There are due dates and deadlines. There are grades. There is a revision process, but it is not infinite.

High-quality writing does take time; however, the time required is moderated by the quality and the quantity of work invested. Ten minutes of average work is not one-third as effective as 30 minutes of serious, dedicated, and superior work. Ms. Finney's ninth-graders learn a lot about work as they simultaneously learn about writing. Some of the students may think that the work is as extreme as the writing.

Notice also that the students and Ms. Finney invested their time and effort in thinking, writing, more thinking, and revision of the writing. They did not spend time on debates and complaints over "when will we ever need to know this?" or "what's this got to do with real life?" The topic the students wrote about was straight from the ninth-grade social studies curriculum—"Students will know the content of the Bill of Rights; students will know how to apply the Bill of Rights to real-life situations; students will know how the Supreme Court applies the Bill of Rights as it decides cases to which the Bill of Rights is relevant."

The topic also is from the real lives that students are living right now. Few topics are of more interest to students than their life as it is being lived now. Extreme writing captures that interest as an essential resource in developing high-quality writing skills, products, and results.

Ms. Finney has developed a writing revision process that works for her and the students in her classes. Teachers of elementary school students, teachers of middle school students, and other teachers of high school students may create different revision processes; however, there will be a similar goal—to develop high-quality writing skills and high-quality writing results through a process that takes students through a sequence of thinking, writing, and revisions with progress made at each step.

The use of extreme writing topics that connect (1) the wholesome knowledge, talents, and interests of students, (2) the school's curriculum, and (3) each writing activity will help the teacher and the student concentrate on the thinking and the writing without losing time to the "why do we have to do this?" or to the "I'm not doing that. What's in it for me?" defiance.

## FOR TEACHERS ONLY: TEACHING INSIGHT 10

Do students see you write? Do students get to read your writing? Do you sometimes complete an assignment yourself just as you expect the students to complete it and then, after the students' papers are graded and returned, read your paper to the students?

Do teachers write articles for the school newspaper? Do teachers post writing on their webpage as part of the school website? When you create an assignment for your students, do you write the information you give the students in a way that exemplifies the type of writing the students are expected to do?

Have you written an article for a teacher organization's publication or for a publication about teaching? Do you have a blog? Have you written an article for the local newspaper?

Do students get to see that writing is as important to you as you hope writing will be to the students?

## FOR PRINCIPALS ONLY: ADMINISTRATOR INSIGHT 7

Do students and teachers see you write? Do students and teachers read your writing? With increased emphasis on development of writing skills by all students, how can a principal lead by example?

You could ask teachers to give you a copy of writing assignments they give to students. You could do some of the assignments and visit classes to see how your work on the assignment and the students' work on the assignment were similar or different. You could stagger this so you work with different classes, different grade levels, and different subjects.

You could write an article for a school administrator publication, for the local newspaper, for the school newspaper, for the school website, or for a blog.

You could host an electronic town hall where teachers and students can ask questions via e-mail. Your responses combine leadership, communication, and the importance of writing.

Leading by example involves no new laws, regulations, taxes, or policies, yet can surpass all of those in positive results.

## WRITING MECHANICS

Spelling counts, so count spelling. Punctuation counts, so count punctuation. Word choices count, so count word choices. Spelling, punctuation, and word choices are some of the measurements of quality writing.

In athletics the measurements could be percentage of free throws made, batting average, yards per carry by a football player, goals allowed by a soccer goalkeeper, time taken by a track participant running 100 yards, or average number of errors made by a softball team per game.

In music competitions the measurements could be the scores given by judges who evaluate a band, an orchestra, or a choral group. In getting a driver's license the measurement is the score on the driving test. In part-time jobs for high school students the measurement could be the hourly wage.

In many parts of life that elementary, middle school, and high school students are very interested in, committed to, enthusiastic about, and fascinated by, measurements are common. Similar measurements can be used in school academics to give details. Grades on report cards are one type of overall measurement. Grades on tests, quizzes, and other assignments are more detailed measurements. Within the grade on a writing assignment can be specific measurements of writing mechanics, such as spelling, punctuation, and word choice, among others.

Spelling: it is right or it is wrong. There is no creative spelling that is clever enough or close enough to be accepted. "But why does spelling count against me? You knew what word I meant." The extreme writing teacher has many possible replies, depending on the wholesome knowledge, interests, and talents of his or her students.

"The basketball referee knows you meant to hit the shot, but if it bounced off the rim and does not go through the hoop, the referee cannot give you points."

"The dentist knows that you meant to eat less sugary food, but she still had to fill that cavity you told me about."

"The police officer knew you meant to stay within the speed limit, but you said to people in class that you were 20 miles per hour over the speed limit."

"The marching band judges knew that everyone meant to be in step properly and play the right notes, but they saw a few minor mistakes. Your band director said that was the difference between first and second place."

"The paper you wrote was very interesting. It was all about how unfair you thought it was to get punished at home for not doing your chores and for letting your grades drop. You meant to do better, but the results show that the chores were not completed and the grades were far below your best."

While there are exceptions, most words in the English language have one correct way to be spelled. Spelling counts. If a teacher creates certificates to give as awards for outstanding work done by students but misspells the name of the award and the name of the student on the certificate, the errors will be noticed and the certificate will mean less than it could have. Spelling counts. Spelling cannot be negotiated. Spelling has to be learned. Elementary school students might reverse a letter and write *garben* instead of *garden*. Middle school students could confuse to, too, and two. High school students may inaccurately use their, there, and they're. Spelling counts, spelling is noticed, spelling matters.

Spelling counts, so count spelling. Count as in points earned for no spelling errors and points lost due to spelling errors. Count in ways that get the attention of your students, such as elementary school students earn privileges for papers with no spelling errors while other students do extra spelling work to gain mastery. Middle school students may benefit from the old-fashioned methods of making their own set of flash cards for vocabulary words and spelling words followed by a weekly spelling test. High school students do not necessarily grow into accurate spelling. Sixteen-year-olds can misspell words, but can learn to accurately spell those words.

Make spelling part of the grade for each writing assignment. "But I don't want to discourage their creativity or their willingness to write." Does the band director who insists that each note be played correctly— a B note is not a C note—overlook incorrect, misplayed notes for fear of discouraging the students' willingness to play music? No; to develop musical skills includes accurately playing each note. To tolerate incorrect notes is to tolerate unacceptable musicianship. To tolerate incorrect spelling is to tolerate limited literacy.

Punctuation counts; so: count, punctuation. How does that prior sentence look and read in terms of punctuation? You are correct. That sentence needs help. Think of wholesome knowledge, talents, and interests of your students that could have similarities with and connections to the importance of accurate punctuation. The list below is a beginning, but please expand it.

1. The intermission during a play or a long movie is similar to a period that separates sentences.
2. Pennies, nickels, dimes, quarters, and half-dollars are to a dollar what punctuated phrases are to a sentence.

3. A loud crowd at an athletic event cheers the way an exclamation point adds vitality to a sentence.
4. A person pauses while speaking as a comma puts a pause in a sentence.
5. The four seasons punctuate a year.
6.
7.
8.
9.
10.

Word choices count, so count word choices. A good place to begin is by eliminating the nonwords *thing* and *stuff*. That thing is getting in the way of my stuff. You have so much stuff squeezed into the closet, there is no room for my things. What? Those sentences evaporate with no substance to keep them in place.

Students' vocabulary can easily fall into limited patterns with a few all-purpose nouns matching up with a few all-purpose verbs to create no-purpose sentences.

"Why should we hire you for this job?" "Why should we give you a full scholarship to our college?" "Why should you be given the new bicycle you requested for your birthday?" "Why should we spend money to get the new clothes you are so interested in?" Such questions should not be answered with "Well, you know, it would, like, um, it would be really neat if you did that." Word choices count. Word choices matter.

"You should hire me for the job because I am fully qualified, because my achievement of being an Eagle Scout shows that I am responsible and dependable, my good grades at school show that I work hard, and my leadership roles in community service projects show my good people skills." Have students contrast that answer with the generic "Well, you know, it would, like, um, it would be really neat if you did that." They can analyze the impact of word choices.

A middle school student would like to attend a computer camp for a week during the summer, but her family cannot afford the cost of the camp. A school counselor hears of the student's interest and tells her that a national computer manufacturing company provides five camp scholarships that pay for all costs and include a free laptop computer for each of the five scholarship recipients. The scholarship application includes a letter the student must write about how computers help her with classes at school.

"Computers are neat. They are fun and cool. They help me because it is not as much work if you use computers and stuff."

"All of my classes use computers. The greatest benefit to me is that the computer puts me in touch with all of the information I need. I showed my grandmother how the computer takes me all around the world, and she was amazed. The computer programs help me concentrate on learning instead of searching. I think more because the computer searches so fast. Instead of going from library to library in hours, I go from one big idea to another big idea in seconds."

Those two paragraphs show the impact of word choices. Are computers neat, fun, and cool? Will those words earn a camp scholarship? Are computers something a granddaughter can teach her grandmother about? Does that selection of words that express a compelling thought present a stronger reason to award a camp scholarship?

Word choice drill and practice can be done in a few minutes as one short activity in any class. Math has a very exact language, with terms such as *triangle, sum, square, parallel lines, exponent,* or *standard deviation* each having a clear and certain meaning. *Triangle* and *square* cannot be used interchangeably. "The three soccer players were told to always realize the triangle they formed on the field. One player had the ball and passed it as another player was moving to receive the next pass, as the first player moved further away to receive the second pass. The soccer field is shaped as a square with parallel lines at either end or either side of the field. In a soccer game the sum of players on the field is 11." Students could identify the correct use of math words in that paragraph and could improve the inaccurate word choices. The students could also include more words or replace existing words to make word choice improvements.

How long should a writing assignment be? A major determinant is the objective of the writing assignment. If students are writing questions that will be e-mailed to next week's guest speaker, one sentence will be a sufficient length for each question. When students sign a thank-you letter that is sent to that guest speaker, the letter will be several paragraphs long with proper formatting of a formal letter. When the students write their impressions of, reactions to, and overall evaluation of the presentation made by the guest speaker, one page of writing could be reasonable. When students select one of the many topics the guest speaker discussed and do thorough research on that topic, the resulting writing could easily become three to five or more typed, double-spaced pages of content. The purpose of the writing is an important factor in the length of the writing.

Another significant factor is expressed in this formula: length = $f$(idea), meaning that the length of the writing is a function of the idea or ideas the writing will communicate. The questions for the guest speaker each express one idea and can be communicated in one effective sentence. The thorough research done to analyze many aspects of the idea in that question makes this a longer writing project of three to five pages or more. The combined factors of purpose and idea will determine the proper length of a writing task.

Writing as the result of revision and more revision is writing that can continually improve. Superior writing is the result of a detailed, disciplined, sometimes laborious, but potentially meaningful series of thoughts, ideas, words, sentences, paragraphs, pages, revisions, new thoughts, new ideas, more precise or more potent words, more effective sentences, better-designed paragraphs, and higher-quality pages. The results can be very fulfilling for the student and the teacher, for the writer and the reader. With those thoughts in mind, the next topic is writing as liberation.

# 8

# WRITING AS LIBERATION

"**T**here are two types of days at school. Some days at school are bad. Other days at school are worse. No days at school are good. I'm going to tell you all about school. You will not like some of what I tell you. Doing this is not my idea. I'm a senior in high school. The second semester started yesterday. The principal and my guidance counselor met with me yesterday. What they told me is the worst possible news a high school senior can hear." Jason's thoughts were very clear as he talked to himself on the way to the principal's office for the second time in two days.

"Jason, as you know, you will not graduate in May with your class. Your first-semester grades were awful, the worst you have ever had." The principal, Mr. Porter, was no-nonsense, just the facts. "Maybe my counselor could save me," Jason thought.

"Mr. Porter and I have considered one very unusual option." Ms. Hart said, "but it would require more work from you, Jason, than you have ever done in school."

"Please, tell me what I have to do. I know I should have made good grades, but if there is any way I can still graduate in May with the other seniors, I'll do whatever you tell me. I thought a lot since we talked yesterday. Thank you for meeting with me again now. Just tell me what I have to do, please."

Mr. Porter and Ms. Hart looked at each other and seemed to send some grownup signal that meant Jason was probably going to reject the one option they could offer.

"Jason, you will write a book about school. From what Ms. Hart and I can tell, you have outstanding academic potential, but you barely do any work. We sincerely would like to read your thoughts about school. You also must pass all classes this semester with a C or better grade in each class, take one class at zero hour, which is one hour before the school day begins, and make a B or better grade in it, and you must take one class online with a B or better grade."

"Write a book. Are they serious? Mr. No-Nonsense, just the facts Principal Porter was always serious. Ms. Hart knows that I hate to read, well, I hate to read schoolbooks. I'll read anything on a computer screen or in a text message," thought Jason.

He gave the only answer available to a person in his position. "Yes, sir, I'll be glad to write a book. How long does it have to be?"

The words from Mr. Porter shocked him: "250 pages, typed, double-spaced. Due May 1."

Ms. Hart added this encouragement. "Jason, today is January 6. You have over 100 days until the book is due. Complete two or three pages per day and you could graduate with your class in May. For this Friday, you will turn in to me a very detailed outline of your book or the first few pages of your book. Any questions?"

None that he could ask without getting suspended from school. He used all of the self-control and acting ability he could find. "No. No questions at all. Thank you both very much. I will write a book you will be amazed by. And in May I'll shake your hands as I am given my high school diploma. Thank you. Happy new year."

Jason was given a note to take to his first-period teacher to excuse his late arrival in class. He went straight to that class, which was about psychology. His thoughts were on writing a book, not on theories of how children learn to speak. The teacher called on him once to explain which theory he thought made the most sense. "Well, I have my own theory. I think children learn to speak through a desire to be heard. Children notice that adults talk, so children seek to join in. That's their motivation to begin talking."

Graduating from high school in May was Jason's motivation to begin writing. He hated writing. "I will probably never write another word in my life after I finish page 250 of my book, but I will finish this. In fact, Mr. Porter and Ms. Hart will never forget the book I write. They will probably never tell another student to write a book," Jason thought,

A detailed outline or writing a few pages was his first task. That outline sounded to him like something his seventh-grade English teacher had made him do. She got so excited about the unit on outlines, and he could never figure out why she was so excited; he did his outline without one moment of excitement. Maybe outlines were a big deal a long time ago when his seventh-grade English teacher was a seventh-grade English student. Jason's score on the seventh-grade English outline was 71, which was a D grade. He could have done it over to improve the grade to 80, which was a C. He did not do it over, figuring you pass with a D grade, so why bother?

Grades are strange. School is strange. No wonder people are happy when they graduate. Jason knew he'd be more than happy when he graduated and would be the one graduate who beat the system. "Nobody thinks I'll write this book. Well, graduation will be freedom from this school, so writing this book is my ticket to freedom. This may not be the book that Mr. Porter and Ms. Hart expect, but it will be 250 pages of words they will never forget. The price of my freedom is 250 pages. Nothing will keep me from finishing this. This writing will set me free." Jason's initial thoughts would soon fill his book's first page.

Jason will be liberated from high school when he completes the requirements, including writing a book about high school, which the principal and the guidance counselor explained to Jason as the conditions for graduation. Jason may be surprised as he writes the book to encounter ideas that go from his mind to the words that fill the 250 pages. Mr. Porter and Ms. Hart will find some provocative ideas in the 250 pages. Suggestions could emerge from Jason's book that, when implemented, would actually make the high school a better place. Writing can liberate Jason in more ways than he anticipates. Jason's readers, as they interact with Jason's ideas, may also find some stretching of their own thinking, which could have a liberating impact as existing rules or procedures at the high school are questioned and challenged.

Mr. Porter and Ms. Hart might have used another approach with Jason. "Your first-semester grades were awful. You have to repeat the first semester at the same time that you complete, successfully, the second semester. Here are five sets of 50 worksheets per class from the first semester. One set of 50 worksheets is due February 1, and another February 15, another March 1, another March 15, and the last set on April 1. If you do all of those well enough to get credit for the first se-mester, you could still pass for the year, but you also have to pass every class this semester. Check in with Ms. Hart every Monday morning at 8:00 a.m. for the rest of the year to update her on the worksheets and to meet with her about your grades for the second semester. This plan is your only option for graduating in May."

Five sets of 50 worksheets per set would not liberate anyone from anything. Two hundred and fifty worksheets of generic blanks to fill in, word searches to sleep through, and questions to guess at would not educate or liberate Jason. Two hundred and fifty pages of his thinking, his ideas, his perceptions, his insights, his experiences, his successes, and his failures at high school could educate him and could liberate him. The readers of the worksheets will gain nothing from reading them or from grading them. The readers of the book will be impacted, will think, will learn, will know if their innovative plan to help Jason graduate worked or not.

Writing at school, writing for school, even writing about school can serve many purposes. Jason initially sees the book as his ticket to high school graduation. He will realize, as he thinks and writes, that thinking and the writing that expresses that thinking can be wonderfully liberat-ing. We will visit Jason again later in this book.

Despite the reality of limitations, people often resent being told that there are limits. How many high school students in the United State see themselves as future professional athletes? How many actual jobs exist in this county for professional athletes? The job market for professional athletes is a realistic limitation. "You can become anything you decide to become" is a sincere statement of encouragement expressed by many adults to many children or teenagers. For application to writing, empha-sis on the "decide to become" part will follow.

Every person who has become a medical doctor, a successful business owner, a great parent, a church leader, a public-office holder, or a professional athlete began the journey to that achievement with an idea. Ideas that get put into writing have a better chance of becoming reality, because what gets written down gets measured, and what gets measured gets done.

Welcome to a thinking and writing adventure called Extreme History. This experience is in the extreme writing family. The details of the assignment follow.

## EXTREME WRITING IN HISTORY

### Extreme History—U.S. History Project

Everything will be G-rated, legal, and ethical.

1. You select the career that is of most interest to you.
2. You will research the history of this career. Emphasize how this type of work has developed during the U.S. history era 1607–2009, or as much of that time period as is accurate. Note: some careers may be more twentieth century or twenty-first century, but research what events led to these careers in earlier times. Summarize your findings with at least eight facts expressed in sentences using your words, not using Internet printouts or copied pages.
3. Explain how this career/work impacted U.S. history. Include at least two specific ways that this career/work has impacted the United States throughout our history. "It made things better" is a nonexample.
4. Who are some major people who have contributed to this work and to the knowledge and achievements associated with this career? List at least two prominent people and how/what they contributed to this career.
5. You will identify the specific skills required for success in this career. List at least four and tell why each skill you list is vital to success in this career. "Be nice" is a nonexample.
6. You will identify the educational requirements for admission into this career. Include high school, volunteer/community work that

applies, college, graduate/professional school, certifications, tests, professional organizations that must admit you, and more. Use at least one college, vocational/technical, or armed-forces website, cite it, and quote it.

7. Your 10-year plan: from junior year of high school to actually doing this work. See below:

| Year: | To be accomplished: |
|---|---|
| 1 | Junior year of high school |
| 2 | Senior year of high school |
| 3 | |
| 4 | |
| 5 | |
| 6 | |
| 7 | |
| 8 | |
| 9 | |
| 10 | |

8. You will use at least four different sources, at least two of which are non-Internet and at least one of which is a person who currently is involved in this career. Cite the sources on a bibliography page, and when you used them.

9. You will not turn in material printed from the Internet or copied from books; rather you will turn in your typed summary of the research you did using your words spelled correctly and punctuated correctly with real sentences.

10. You have format options. Include all required content, but a creative format—poster, magazine, brochure, illustrations—or a standard text or a combination is fine.

This Extreme History project is due Monday, November 10, at the start of class ready to turn in—printed and stapled, with your name on it—done completely and correctly.

Similar to many subjects in the school curriculum, U.S. history can appear to students as so distant in time and in ways of living that it has no connection to their real life today. The extreme history project connects U.S. history and the current career ambition of students. The result of this thinking, research, reading, interviewing, and writing project has always been that students learned much more than they expected to learn. Another valuable result has been that students either became more convinced of their interest in a certain career goal or they realized that their original career goal is not the kind of work they are as suited for as they originally thought.

The extreme history writing assignment is liberating. Every student is free to explore the career interest that is most important to them individually. Every student comes across information, advice, and insights in the "I never knew that" or "I never realized that" revelation category, thus freeing them from the restriction of insufficient awareness. Some students are liberated from a career misperception that could have meant years headed toward work that was not a good match for their interests, talents, values, concerns, and life goals. Other students strengthen their resolve to overcome any obstacles because they have clearly confirmed their career intention, which frees them from distractions, doubts, or uncertainty. Extreme history provides a good example of the liberating power of extreme writing.

Thus far the human being cannot run a three-minute mile, but people can think about it and can write about it. Thus far the human being cannot travel in time to the past or to the future, but people can think about time travel and people can write about time travel. It is reported that one billion people are malnourished or undernourished daily on planet Earth, but people can think about feeding everyone who hungers, people can write about feeding everyone who hungers, with the result of such thinking and writing being that some people will get involved in reducing hunger.

People can think about and write about what could or should exist. Such writing liberates the writer and the reader from the grip of current restrictions on achievement. Breakthrough achievements begin with magnificent ideas expressed energetically in writing that intrigues, inspires, and compels. Before astronauts landed on the moon such an achievement had been thought about and written about.

Writing can appear to be as routine as completing a survey about brands of laundry detergent a person prefers. Yet to the market research expert who analyzes the comments from those surveys, the ideas and the words of the surveys become product improvements that give the brand a competitive edge in the marketplace. This liberation comes in being freed from the confines of the status quo because new insights from consumers have opened or expanded the thinking at a consumer product company.

The detergent survey is mentioned as an example of apparently routine writing being transformed into liberating action. Some school writing activities may appear to be routine initially, but liberation is within writing that is uplifted from the routine to the emancipating. What is an example? and How is this done? are two very reasonable questions.

Example: a teacher begins each sixth-grade Language Arts class with a two-minute written thought-starter. Students know that when the bell rings to begin class, they are to have pencil or pen on paper writing a short response to the thought-starter topic. One Monday the thought-starter was "Write a conversation between a sentence and a paragraph." Many students struggled to write anything, but finally got a few comments on paper. A few very creative students could have kept writing their sentence and paragraph conversation all day. The teacher, Ms. Cambridge, led a quick discussion about the thought-starter and then moved into other activities about sentences and paragraphs.

Tuesday's thought-starter was changed. The original plan was "What did the comma say to the exclamation point?" but Ms. Cambridge decided that was too confusing and too much like Monday's topic, which so many students had trouble with. The revised topic was "Why do we have punctuation?" This is clear, simple, straightforward, and direct, so Ms. Cambridge anticipated no problems.

The written responses were as limited as the topic. "Because it is the law of Language Arts." "So words don't bunch up." "So teachers have something to grade." This was not working. The thought-starter was supposed to provide a structured routine and was intended to truly start the thinking. Ms. Cambridge was beginning to conclude that the results were unthinking, meaning that brains were being turned off by the thought-starter.

On Wednesday before class Ms. Cambridge heard a few students talking about a contest sponsored by a local radio station. The top prize was front-row seats and backstage passes to a concert that every student wanted to attend. That contest and the concert excitement gave Ms. Cambridge an idea, an inspiration. The class would have a contest, with students submitting topics for thought-starters.

The creativity this contest liberated was unlimited. The interest in thought-starters skyrocketed. The results from the thought-starters increased because the students actually started thinking at the beginning of each class with the intellectual vigor that Ms. Cambridge had intended.

As Ms. Cambridge evaluated the impact of using the student-designed thought-starters, she gave much attention to how much it meant to each student when his or her thought-starter topic was used. Maybe that was to be expected, but what was unexpected in this process was how much harder all of the students worked to respond to student-designed thought-starters and how eager they were to read their responses aloud in class. The students were eager to impress each other. There was something important about having an audience.

Up until now, Ms. Cambridge collected the thought-starters and read them, usually collecting them on Friday, for the entire week's worth of five writings. She used to have a short discussion in class daily about each thought-starter, but few students participated. Now, student participation was the best ever, and very Socratically, Ms. Cambridge led that participation from thought-starter commentary into the rest of the day's lesson plan. The thought-starter increasingly was the learning starter and lesson starter, not merely a chore or a routine that had to be done because someone, somewhere had required it or recommended it; well, Ms. Cambridge was not really sure how it had begun, but she knew how it was working now.

More and more Ms. Cambridge emphasized the idea of writing with the reader in mind. Her students were encouraged to think about writing as an interactive communication method instead of just putting words on paper to get an assignment finished. One purpose of writing is to have an impact on the reader. For these sixth-graders that perspective on writing was a new reason to write better. Ms. Cambridge used a letter she found in a box at home to communicate an idea that writing for the reader can be very important. It was a letter her father had written to Santa Claus when he was eight years old.

*2442 Trather Road*
*Lexington, KY*
*December 24, 1962*

*Dear Santa,*

*Sorry I did not write sooner. I just did not find time to.*
*This year I want some Lego, talking Cecil, Hasbro-Bowl-a-tron, Megnatable, please.*

*Yours truly,*
*Kevin Cambridge*

*P.S. Thank you for the presents you brought me last year. They were very nice.*

The sixth-graders then put themselves in the place of an eight-year-old who was writing a letter to Santa Claus. They also had to write letters to a local church or charity asking for that group to reach out to people who needed extra help at the holiday season. The intended readers of the two letters were in the minds of the students as they wrote. The content of the letters varied, depending on who would read the letter. The Santa Claus connection related to student knowledge. The two different letters taught the importance of different writing for different readers/audiences.

There was one more unexpected result. The students asked if they could really send their letter to the local churches or charities they had selected. Ms. Cambridge checked with the principal and was given approval. Much to the students' delight, one local church and one local charity teamed up with the class to create a food drive and a toy drive at the Thanksgiving and Christmas seasons. For these students writing was real, and writing had been liberated from a task for a class to involvement in the community.

Consider a high school that announced in April that there was increasing concern about problems caused with cell-phone use at school. The policy had been that phones must be off and out of sight from the time a student arrived on campus to the end of the instructional school day. Classes were disrupted with phone calls and text messages. Legal issues were emerging as students used the camera feature on their phone to publicize people who sought no publicity. The content of some websites that students had access to via their phones undermined the effort of the school and the school district to block improper websites from the school's computers.

The school officials were asking for input about a proposed new policy—cell phones and all other electronic devices would not be allowed on the campus or in the school building at all. Most students had some very strong opinions on this topic. Mr. Willmore, experienced teacher of high school English to juniors and seniors, saw this as a perfect opportunity for his eleventh-grade students to apply their writing skills. The assignment he gave them generated a very enthusiastic response.

"A new cell-phone and electronic-device policy has been proposed for our high school. The new policy bans all such devices from campus on school days. The school officials have requested input about that proposed policy. This topic is getting much attention at school and throughout the community. Your assignment is to write four different letters that express your thoughts about the proposed policy. The four letters will be directed to the principal, the school newspaper's opinion page, the local newspaper's letter-to-the-editor page, and to the faculty. Think of the impact you intend to have on each of the four audiences/readers and design each letter to achieve each impact."

Mr. Willmore's students were more than ready, willing, and eager to complete this assignment. Mr. Willmore's challenge was to guide the students so their writing was as effective as possible rather than as explosive as possible. The opinions were very strong. "We have the right to our cell phones. Cell phones are legal." The most productive way to put the opinions into writing would include conviction, energy, and tact. Some revisions would be necessary, especially in search of tact. Mr. Willmore knew his students would comply with the perpetual requirement that everything in class had to be "G-rated, legal, and ethical." He had taught the students well and built a classroom community with each of his classes. The students knew that Mr. Willmore would do anything for them, but that the expected reciprocity for the teacher's total commitment to the students was the students' total cooperation with Mr. Willmore.

The topic of this assignment had a very direct, immediate, and personal connection with the wholesome knowledge, talents, and interests of students. Debates would occur about how wholesome cell phones and other electronic devices are at school, but that exchange of ideas itself could be wholesome. The teachers were insisting on changes in the existing policy, plus complete enforcement of any new policy. Community members, especially parents and guardians of students, generally understood the concerns of school administrators and teachers, but kept saying that they need the convenience and assurance of being in touch with their children via cell phones. The local newspaper had two news stories and an editorial on this topic. The principal and other school administrators knew that cell phones were increasingly causing problems at school and that something had to be done.

Mr. Willmore's students wrote their four letters and then repeatedly revised the letters. An assistant principal visited the class to read the letters and to offer perspective. That visit was followed by another round of revisions to the letters. The principal visited the class and was given the letters that were addressed to him. He and the students had a very spirited and polite discussion about the proposed policy. The principal sincerely appreciated the time, thought, and effort the students had invested in the writing. He found some areas of disagreement with the prevailing student opinions and his own thoughts, but he also gained some ideas that might work their way into the final version of the proposed policy.

Some student writing did appear in the student newspaper. The tone and content of those letters were casual, conversational, and blunt. Some student writing did appear in the local community's newspaper. The tone and content of those letters were formal, diplomatic and respectful while presenting the same opinions as were communicated in the student newspaper.

The letters to the faculty members were sent via e-mail to save paper. There were some replies from teachers. The students began to realize that the power of writing surpassed some of their previous conclusions. Writing really could make a difference. Writing can liberate and direct ideas that can become action. A few students raised questions about whether adjusting their writing for a variety of readers meant they were manipulating their writing and were not true to the purity of their thoughts.

For those students who raised these ethical questions, much respect was given for their concern about integrity. The explanation that was most convincing came from a student. "Look, it's like when we go to the prom. We dress up. It's not fake. It's a real prom. We're still ourselves, just dressed fancy and all that. If it's a Friday night football game we wear regular clothes. You pick the right clothes for each event, but you are the same person. We pick the right words for each reader, but our opinion about cell phones is the same no matter how formally or casually we dress our opinion in the way we write it."

Most writing done by students at schools is turned in to, read by, and graded by the teacher and then returned to the student. That writing sequence is an important part of attaining writing skills.

Some of those student-to-teacher writing tasks may have a variety in the assignment that directs the student to write as if the paper would be read by the president, by a corporate executive, by a celebrity, by the author of a book the students read, or by a historical figure. When the writing is actually going to be shared with, sent to, read by, and responded to by someone other than the teacher, there is an extra "this really matters" dynamic. With some phone calls, e-mails, and networking, teachers can arrange for people in the local community to read and to respond to student writing as allowed by the requirements in school policies. This can inspire deeper student commitment while also building new partnerships of school and community.

Writing that is finite, something to finish and turn in, done to avoid a failing grade, busywork, or otherwise just an item to mark off the day's to-do list, is not liberating. That type of writing serves to complete a task, put that task in the past, and move on from that task.

Writing that is liberating is writing that connects one idea to another idea, one idea to an action the idea evokes or inspires, one part of life to another part of life. Extreme writing is one way to bring the attribute of and the inspiration of connectedness or connectiveness to writing. Because extreme writing connects the wholesome knowledge, talents, and interests of students with writing, extreme writing matters more than writing that simply fits a 10-minute hole during a class period.

Writing that liberates is part of a continuum of writing that a teacher designs very intentionally to logically and academically reach goals, yet to also transcend goals. The writing a teacher has her students do in August should serve immediate and long-term academic purposes. The students master sentences in August so they can master paragraphs in

September so they can master essays in October. This is an example of the instructional and academic logical flow of writing goals. As those instructional goals are reached, liberating goals are simultaneously reached only to be replaced by the pursuit of new personal, individualized goals.

While sentences, paragraphs, and essays are mastered in an accumulating and progressive approach, thoughts and ideas are accumulating and progressing. There is an October revelation. "I get it" is spoken or otherwise proclaimed by a student whose extreme writing teacher has liberated one more scholar, one more thinker, one more mind to create ideas and to express those ideas in academically valid ways to show mastery of the curriculum and in personally meaningful ways to show emerging mastery of life itself.

To increase student commitment to and success in writing, making the writing connect with and therefore matter to the real life of the student right now is effective. To further increase student commitment to, success in, and rewards from writing, make each separate writing activity fit with all other separate writing activities into one continuously developing totality of writing. This totality combines writing skills, ideas, personal reflection, thinking, individualized contemplation, mastery of writing mechanics, and appreciative awareness that "I think therefore I write therefore I live better" is true, meaningful, real, always available, and endlessly liberating. How's that for a philosophy of extreme writing in particular and of writing in general?

Student writing can sometimes liberate a teacher. For example, consider a group of five students who incorrigibly caused problems in a high school class. On certain days these students made very sensible comments about the topic being discussed or asked very insightful questions about the topic. A few moments after making one of those impressive comments or asking one of the good questions, the same students could be silly, impolite, disruptive, and defiant. The teacher used every possible discipline method and reward method. Progress was limited and was temporary.

Eventually the teacher required each of the five persistent offenders to answer in writing some questions related to their misbehaviors. The answer one student troublemaker gave to one question liberated the teacher from not fully realizing what he had been dealing with to a completely new awareness.

The students were given several questions, including the following: "In the space below, explain what you are thinking when you misbehave and your misbehavior causes the teacher to have to spend time dealing with your misbehavior. Be sure to explain why you think you have to steal that time the teacher should use for teaching but has to use to deal with your misbehavior."

The response written by one student was "I don't consider what I do to be misbehavior." Disrupting class with silly, rude comments. Defying instructions from the teacher. Ignoring instructions to read. Ignoring repeated instructions to turn around, face the front, stay awake, and listen. This steady stream of misdemeanors resulted in many discipline actions imposed by the teacher, the student's parent, and school administrators; however, the student could claim that he does not consider what he does to be misbehavior.

The teacher persisted with that student from the start to the end of the school year. The teacher did change his tactics after the student's statement liberated the teacher from all prior perspectives. The teacher had thought that the student's misbehavior could be corrected with the right amount of determined effort by the teacher, the parent, and school administrators along with the certainty of discipline actions following each misbehavior. The misbehaviors continued despite all actions taken. One different tactic was to stop using any appeal to reason to change the student's thinking; rather, to every misbehavior action there needed to be an equal and opposite discipline action.

There is still hope that the student will change his thinking, but once he made his teacher aware in writing of his thinking, it was obvious that actions with that student needed to change. The student finished the school year, got a credit for the class, and was given something to think about. In reply to his excuse, his rationalization, his statement that eludes ethics and the impact of a conscience—"I don't consider what I do to be misbehavior"—he was asked, in writing, "then why has it resulted in many referrals and in discipline action by associate principals? Because whether you think so or not, it is misbehavior."

The teacher will follow up with the student during the next school year. The student will not expect that. "You aren't my teacher this year." True, not for a class, but for other learning. After a summer, with some additional maturity in the student and with the reality of high school graduation approaching, the student may be willing to reconsider his written statement. He'll be given a copy of it and a chance to revise it. The hope is that his revised thinking expressed in revised writing and manifested in revised, much improved behavior will liberate that student from the limits he has thus far imposed on himself.

## EXTREME THINKING

### Scholars Know

Scholars know that . . .
- There is more to listening than hearing.
- There is more to reading than seeing words.
- There is more to paying attention than avoiding distractions.
- There is more to watching than looking.
- There is more to a test than answering questions.
- There is more to homework than completing something to hand in.
- There is more to studying than merely doing the assignment.
- There is deep thinking, there are profound ideas, there are insightful questions, there is wholesome curiosity, there is mental interactivity, there is mastery of old knowledge and creation of new knowledge.
- There is total concentration.
- There is reading again what you have already read, but thinking about it anew.
- There is reading another book when a paragraph or a page from an article or a book just cannot tell all that can be known, all that should be learned, and all that could be explored.
- There is thinking followed by putting the thoughts into written words, followed by reading those words, followed by thinking anew and thinking better because the brain, mind, and the written words interact.
- There can be a healthy, motivational, inspirational dissatisfaction with good enough.
- There can be a relentless challenge to the very good that takes a scholar beyond the very good.
- There is an insistence on better than ever followed by a relentless pursuit of better than that.

- There is a brain combined with a mind, which together have no limits.
- Scholars know that the brain and the mind are unlimited. Scholars set no limits on thinking and on learning. Avoid limits on thinking and on learning—be a scholar. If you are not a scholar yet, do what scholars do. What is that? Read this essay again so you can know what scholars do and so you can then do what scholars do. There is no limit to how many people can become scholars. That means there is no limit to how many people can think and learn without limits.
- What scholars know is also what scholars believe. Scholars believe that learning is not a task to be quickly completed and done with. Scholars believe that learning is to the mind and to the brain what a pulse is to the heart and what breathing is to the lungs. Scholars believe that unlimited learning is unlimited living. Because there is more to be learned, there is more to be lived. Scholars believe in their ability to learn and in their need to learn. Scholars know. Scholars believe. Scholars get the most out of life because they learn the most about life. We can live only what we have learned. We live more completely as we learn more and as we learn more completely.

Extreme writing is one way to develop more scholars and to develop more scholarly accomplishment by students who have already reached or committed to the scholarly approach. Extreme writing does with writing what scholars do with every topic to study and with productive, honorable methods of study—think, express ideas, connect ideas, stretch the brain, liberate the mind, live a meaningful life of purposeful, G-rated, legal, ethical, honorable, important questions, answers, and ideas that take shape through written words and then touch lives and impact life itself.

We return to Jason and the book he is writing as one part of the plan that could qualify him to graduate from high school. The initial part of his book follows. Please read this and then determine what else you think he would include in the rest of the book.

## JASON'S BOOK: CHAPTER ONE

Write this paper or don't graduate from high school. How's that for a choice? Which would you do? I asked my friends about it. Most of them said to just make myself write the paper. A few said I should forget the paper and see what happens. One friend of mine said I should get a lawyer and take on the system.

I decided to write the paper because by the time I wait to see what happens if I don't write it or by the time I get a lawyer, I could finish the paper. I still think that this paper is going to be no fun to write, but it is my ticket to high school graduation. My parents said I could forget my car until I am an official high school graduate with a diploma. I expect them to hand me the car keys right after the principal hands me a high school diploma.

I decided to write something about elementary school and middle school before I start writing about high school. That's logical, isn't it? Elementary school was not bad. Everything was new. By fifth grade I was tired of it and really looked forward to middle school. I had done everything there was to do at elementary school. I could read and write. I stayed out of trouble. I was involved with a campus clean-up group that some fourth-graders began. My teachers were friendly in the way that only teachers who work with little children can be friendly. It's like they are your aunt or uncle or grandparent and they do a lot for you.

Then I went to middle school, and those years were a total waste. We did the same thing every year. Each math teacher taught the same fractions and equations every year. It was so stupid to do that over and over.

We had elective classes in middle school. I wanted to take a class in car repair, but that's for high school students only. By the time I was old enough in high school for car repair classes, my grades were so bad I did not qualify. If they had let me work on cars in middle school, I never would have been a problem for anyone.

We got a new principal in middle school when I was an eighth-grader. She was sent to our school to get everything under control. Too many students had been getting suspended, and a lot of teachers had quit. There was something about test scores at the school being low.

Funny, that new principal stayed only one year. I heard that she went back to her old job at the school district office. The eighth-grade teachers really hated her and told us. Well, actually we overheard them saying really bad things about her. It made me wonder if those teachers spent too much time talking about the principal when they should have been trying to get me in a car repair class.

The truth is that middle school was not worth the time. It was just another form of elementary school. If you had learned what elementary school taught you, you just kept doing that over and over. If you had not learned the elementary school things, you were supposed to finally learn that during middle school.

I was a little bit excited about high school for two reasons—it would not be elementary school and it would not be middle school. I hoped that finally I would get to work on car repair classes, but that did not happen. So here I am writing this book and doing everything else I was told to do so I can graduate from high school.

What do I think of high school? The smart students seem to like it, but for some of them it's not worth four years. They can get the work done in three years, so they should be allowed to do that. Why make them stay for an unnecessary year when they could go on to college sooner?

The almost smart students and the average students just seem to go along and get by. They don't like school and they don't hate school. They see friends. They might play a sport. They usually stay out of trouble. They are ready to get out of here by their senior year, I can tell you that. They've pretty much outgrown high school by then.

The real problem in high school is the group that does not care at all. They fail every class, they yell at teachers. They skip classes. They commit crimes and get arrested and then the judge tells them to go to school. What's the school going to do with them when they should be in jail?

Some of my friends are court involved. They come to school to eat breakfast and lunch. At breakfast they bet each other on who can get suspended from school fastest and for the longest. So they go in the locker room and steal cell phones. Get caught and you are suspended. Don't get caught, you can sell the phone sometimes back to the person it belongs to and tell them if they say anything it will be really bad or tell them you found it but you need a reward for returning it.

I am not court involved. I make bad grades. I get in trouble with teachers. I don't steal. I don't mess with drugs. I just got tired of high school being the same thing class after class, so I gave up, but I'm no criminal.

I have had one or two really good teachers in high school. Actually, most of my teachers tried hard and seemed to work hard, but they had so many of the students who intended to fail that it was never possible to really control class. Why don't schools send that group of students somewhere else?

My best teacher was my tenth-grade computer applications teacher. She knew I was really interested in cars, so everything I needed to learn about computers we set up so it was also about cars. I made a B in that class. It would have been an A, but I'm not very good with getting homework turned in. Still, the teacher told me that I did so well she relied on me sometimes to answer computer questions. It's strange, but that teacher left after my tenth-grade year and became an assistant principal somewhere. I never figured out why she wanted to take a job where she would have to spend all day with students who get in trouble. That's what assistant principals do. They enforce the law. I guess someone has to.

There is a lot more I could say about high school. The halls are way too crowded. The cafeteria is crowded. People smoke in the bathrooms and it smells awful. The criminals steal things and vandalize. The smart students go to the library a lot. Teachers say it used to be a lot better, but it's not so bad. I don't bother people. I just want to finish this and get a diploma and get my car keys. I know this paper has to be longer, so tell me what else to write about and I'll do exactly what you tell me.

*Note to the reader:* If you were the high school principal or counselor who read this paper, what else would you require the student to write about? After identifying the other topics the student must write about, put yourself in the role of the student and write some of the rest of the paper. Jason met with his school counselor, who told him his book had begun well. She suggested that he create four major chapters, with one chapter about each year of high school. What follows is part of Jason's chapter about ninth grade. What would you expect him to say about ninth grade? What would you write about for each of the grades in high school (ninth, tenth, eleventh, and twelfth) if you were Jason?

## JASON'S BOOK: CHAPTER TWO

Ms. Hart is my school counselor. She told me to write a chapter about each year of high school. That sounded easy enough. Here's what I remember about ninth grade. I'll add some of my opinions, too.

A few days before ninth grade actually began, the school invited us to have a ninth-grade practice day. Who needs to practice school when you have already been going to school for eight or nine years? High school is more people, but that's no big deal.

So I went to the practice day and it was a waste. I'm sure that people worked hard to prepare the day, but it was still a waste. How do you practice being a ninth-grader? We heard the principal, the assistant principals, a counselor, and some coaches. I don't play a sport. Why did I have to listen to coaches? I was very interested in cars, but nobody talked about car repair classes and nobody knew anything when I asked about car repair classes. They gave us a school bumper sticker to put on our car. I wanted to fix cars, not put bumper stickers on cars.

Ninth grade got off to a bad start. The first few days we had to sit in homeroom forever because of problems with schedules or something. They blamed the computers. When we got to classes it seemed to me like most of the stuff was just more of the same. English, math, social studies, science. All I wanted was car repair. Why was that so difficult? So it was pretty bad. More of the same old stuff.

A friend of mine talked me into going to the first football game of the year. Lots of the ninth-graders were there and lots of other students, plus tons of parents. What's the big deal about a high school football game? That's easy. It's not football that attracts the crowd. It's the social life. The same thing goes on in the halls at school and even in some classes. Being cool is so important to a lot of the high school students. I guess that's okay, but since cars are cool to me there was no way I was going to be very cool because nobody could find a car class for me.

My first report card was really bad. I blamed it on dumb classes that were boring because we had done this stuff in eighth grade. My parents blamed it on my computer and my cell phone, so they took those away. My school counselor and I met to discuss my grades and stuff. She had no idea who I was. I had no idea who she was. She gave me something about how to study. I asked her about car repair classes and she said I had to be in eleventh grade for that. I asked why. She had no answer. My grades did improve enough to get my computer and my cell phone back. How did I improve my grades? Easy. Most of my teachers just used the book for class. Everything we did was in the book. The night before a test I'd cram the chapter into my brain. I'd remember it long enough to pass the test. Just like middle school. In one class we had to read a novel. The Internet read it for me. There was so much on the Internet about that book, so a few websites and I was okay.

What else happened in ninth grade? Not much. That's the truth, so how am I going to write a 250-page book about high school if not much happened? Well, I could ask other people what they think about high school. If I ask a lot of students and teachers what they think, I could just put those interviews in my book. That should work. I'll go ask some people about what they remember about ninth grade. I'll talk to some ninth-grade teachers, I might even talk to those coaches who talked at our ninth-grade practice day. I'd like to know what they were thinking. Who knows, maybe they were forced to do that and they would rather not but they had to.

The first person I talked to was my friend Samantha. She's my neighbor. She's really smart. We had one class together in ninth grade, but since she takes all of the really hard classes and makes really good grades, that was the last class we had together. I asked her what she liked best about ninth grade.

"Jason, nobody liked ninth grade. What's there to like? It's a huge school. You are lost. There is more work to do. The other students are older. Clubs and sports are for the students who have been there. I mean a ninth-grader can't just walk in and take over. The teachers pile on the work. You might have three or four tests on one day."

My friend Thomas had a neat memory from ninth grade. "Jason don't you remember when we got in trouble in Spanish class? We were late to class two or three days in a row. The teacher would not let us in the next day. The assistant principal found us wandering the halls and figured we needed to learn our lesson. He knew Spanish, so he made us do extra Spanish work. I hated doing the work, but he said it was that or get suspended and my father told me if I ever got suspended I could not get a driver's license. I was never late to Spanish class again."

This book is harder than I thought. Even with interviews it will take forever to write this. I already agreed to write it. This is the only way I can graduate. What happens if my book is no good? What happens if I have to write it over? Maybe I can write a chapter about how difficult it is to write this book. I'm a senior in high school and there's no other way to graduate because I've messed up so many classes.

I always wanted to learn about car repair. They never let me take any car repair class because I was too young or my grades were too low. I'll write the book all about car repair. I'll make this book about what high school should have been for me. Lots of car repair classes every year. When the principal and the counselor read this maybe they'll see what high school should have been for me, plus I'll teach them a lot about car repair. Okay. I can do this.

*Note to the reader:* What might have been Jason's high school experience if his wholesome knowledge of, interest in, and talent with cars could have connected with his high school curriculum?

## FOR PRINCIPALS ONLY: ADMINISTRATOR INSIGHT 8

Jason should have worked much harder in high school. He should have been much more responsible in high school. He put himself in the position where graduation from high school was unlikely. The principal and the counselor created a plan that gave Jason a second chance to graduate from high school on time with his senior class.

What else could have been done to prevent the problem of this high school senior beginning the second semester of the school year with graduation so much in doubt? Could there have been a middle school car repair vocational education program that Jason began in middle school and continued in high school? Could there have been more math and science-class connections with Jason's interest in cars? Imagine the many applications of math and science to the design of, operation of, and repair of cars. Were those applications part of the math and science classes that Jason took in middle school and in high school?

Jason needs to learn about more than cars. The school curriculum is not built upon automobiles; however, since Jason has such a strong and wholesome knowledge of, interest in, and talent with cars, much can be accomplished academically when the school curriculum and car repair team up.

Jason will graduate from high school because the principal and the school counselor gave him a second chance that Jason took seriously, especially when he could connect the second-chance work to his first interest—car repair.

For every Jason who is underperforming and underachieving in every classroom, the power of connecting the school curriculum with the wholesome knowledge, talents, and interests of students can create unlimited achievements while also preventing some other problems such as not graduating from high school.

Jason is going to finish his 250-page book. One reason he will complete the book is a desire to graduate. Another unexpected reason for completing the book with a sense of personal benefit beyond graduating is that Jason has found a way to learn about car repair as he completes the book. Notice the multiple victories—Jason will graduate from high school on time, Jason will learn about car repair, the principal and the counselor identified a creative way to prevent a dropout or a nongraduate, and as the principal and the counselor read Jason's book they can gain ideas about extreme writing that could lead to application of that writing approach at their school across the curriculum and within the curriculum. Please reflect upon how that could be done at your school.

# EPILOGUE

Truth emerges when ideas collide. How do ideas collide? The idea that is thought about is then put in writing. At that point, the thinker interacts with the written expression of the thoughts, and new thinking begins. Consider the following analysis of thinking, of words, and of writing.

## I THINK; THEREFORE, I WRITE

- Words are the building blocks of thoughts, of actions, of life.
- Life requires that we breathe, have a pulse, and use words.
- Loved ones recall the last words of a deceased family member more than the last career achievement or the last financial transaction.
- Life is lived in actions. Actions begin with thoughts. Thoughts begin with words.
- Words elevate us to better lives. Civilization has advanced since written words emerged.
- Words can heal or harm, help or hurt, encourage or offend, create or destroy, love or hate.
- Words are the fiber, the DNA, the elements, the foundation, the material, the cells, the building blocks of writing.

Imagine life without words. That idea is impossible to express without words, which suggests that words are essential.

If words did not exist, what else would be missing from life? Wedding vows. Books. Websites. Instruction manuals. Signs. Names. E-mail. Report cards. Prescriptions for medication. Verbal communication or written communication using words. The Bible. The Constitution. A driver's license. A birth certificate. Newspapers. Diaries, Recipes. Greeting cards. Addresses with names of streets, cities, states, and nations. Radio. Lyrics to songs. Poetry. Conversations.

Carefully chosen words have greater impact than ordinary words. When a gift is thoughtfully selected for a person based on their unique interests, hopes, wants, or needs, the impact of the gift is much greater than an ordinary, generic, all-purpose item. Carefully, thoughtfully written words are gifts of similar impact given by a writer to a reader.

Quality writing requires quality work and a substantial quantity of work. The work a student must do to create masterful writing must far surpass in quality and in quantity the work required to merely make the lowest passing grade. Work—its quality and its quantity—is a variable any student can adjust to his or her advantage, as explained below.

- Some students are smarter than I am, but I make better grades than they do.
- Some students are much smarter than I am, but I will go to a better college than they do.
- Some students are much, much smarter than I am, but I will get a better college scholarship than they will.
- Some students are so much smarter than I am that it's hard to describe, but I will get a better job than they get.
- The biggest difference is that I work.
- I can learn everything a super smart student can learn and more. I just have to work more and work harder.
- There will always be students who are smarter than I am. I cannot change that. No student will ever work more or harder than I work. I can control that. I will do that.

What is the future of writing by students in elementary schools, in middle schools, and in high schools? What is the future of subjects, verbs, sentences, paragraphs, thinking, ideas, and writing? Will verbs be conjugated? Will sentences be diagrammed as a lost art of grammar is discovered anew? Will spelling always count? The following story presents one possibility. The reader is encouraged to think of additional descriptions of the future of writing.

"There are no signs. There are no directions. How do people here find their way around? This is so strange." Barbara was concerned, almost worried. Her twin brother, Paul, tried to be encouraging to his usually confident and optimistic 13-year-old sister.

"Who needs signs with words and names and directions? There are all sorts of other signs. Look. Those people must know where they are going. Let's follow them."

Barbara and Paul followed the crowd, which grew larger and larger. This town was new to the twins and their parents. The Asbury family had moved to the town only one week ago in mid-June after the school year ended in their old hometown. Barbara and Paul liked to wander around their new town, but the absence of street signs and of any other sign did make it confusing.

This small town had an old-fashioned town square. The crowd had gathered there, maybe 150 people. Barbara and Paul listened as one person spoke to the crowd.

"It's been two weeks since all of the signs were taken down in our good city. Don't you agree that it looks better without all of that clutter?" The crowd cheered except for Barbara and Paul, who wondered why removing all signs was such a good idea.

"That's not all. We're getting rid of everything printed, everything with words, that is. No words ever again." The crowd began to chant, "No words. No words."

Barbara and Paul looked at each other with very puzzled and perplexed expressions. Their confusion increased as the speaker continued.

"The street signs have been removed. All signs on stores and other businesses are being removed. No building will be identified with any words on the building, on a sign, or in any other public way with words. The billboards will be gone—no later than July Fourth, Independence Day. We will declare our independence from all of those printed words. For anyone who questions whether this is Constitutional, let there be no doubt. The Constitution protects the freedom to speak and the freedom of the press. Our citizens are still speaking. Our presses are still running. We know what freedom is, and finally we are free from the problems that come from words in print."

The crowd cheered and chanted. Barbara asked Paul, "What's wrong with words?" Two people standing by the twins heard Barbara's questions and replied, "Oh, you are so young, you may not understand, but words cause problems. If we can eliminate words in print, we'll prevent so many conflicts that words cause." The other person noticed that Paul was carrying a book. "Son, those books are next. The library shelves will be empty. In fact the library is changing into an art studio and museum. Pictures are good. Words just cause problems."

The speaker completed the speech. "So, my fellow citizens, some words are gone and more words are going. The newspaper has voluntarily agreed to print pictures only from now on. Since a picture is worth a thousand words, the newspaper will be much shorter. Advertisements in the paper will be pictures only. The businesspeople of our town have already begun to use colors and designs to make each business and building an advertisement easily identified. The phone book will no longer be printed. We're really fancy there. The voice recognition system just hears you say who you are calling, and the call is placed for you. Who knows, maybe we can get rid of numbers too, because they can cause some problems. So, in conclusion, let me say that the printed words are going, going, and are soon to be gone. You have my word on it." The speaker grinned at his pun. The crowd applauded and cheered, except for Barbara and Paul.

Paul wondered, "What do we do now?" He got his answer as the newly renamed City of Pictures (COP) official noticed that Paul was carrying a book. "You there, young man, no books. I'll need to confiscate that, and you'll need to answer some questions."

Barbara tried to help. "But sir, we're new here. We just moved to this town. We didn't know about the new word laws. Our hometown had words everywhere. We're sorry."

The COP official was not convinced. "Young lady, words cause problems. People write mean letters or unfair contracts that are confusing or advertisements that are misleading or letters to the editor that stir up controversy. This town is going to prevent all of the problems that words in print can cause by getting rid of any words in print. So give me that book, and we'll consider this a warning because you are new in town. There will be no more warnings. Now speak into this machine. Tell your name, birthday and year, address and name of adults you live with. The machine records what you say, takes your picture, and processes that. Any other COP official who deals with you will know you have already had one offense."

Barbara and Paul walked home and kept trying to figure out what they had seen and what they had heard. They were still upset about the COP official detaining them. Paul had an idea. "I'm going to write the mayor. I'm going to write the governor. I'm going to write the president."

Barbara had bad news. "No you're not. You would have to put words on paper to write those people."

Paul was determined. "No problem. E-mail will take care of it." As soon as they arrived at their home Paul logged on to his computer, but nothing happened until a picture appeared on the screen. The picture was a huge trash container filled with words, books, newspapers, e-mails, and text messages. In 20 seconds the computer automatically shut down due to what the twins later were told was "unauthorized attempt to use words that might eventually get printed." Since e-mail can be printed out, e-mail use of words in the COP was prohibited. Text messaging was also prohibited. Any text on any website coming into the COP area would be blacked out. Summer moved slowly for Paul and Barbara. COP was a difficult place to get used to or to feel at home in. When school started on August 26, they hoped that life would improve, but it only got more unusual. Their eighth-grade science teacher, Ms. Jordan, explained some changes for this year after she welcomed everyone back to school.

"You have noticed many changes in our city over the summer. There are changes at school also. We will not use anything printed, including books. The library is empty. The computers are gone because text on a screen can become words that are printed. Printed words, it has been decided, can arouse rebellion, cause conflict, create misunderstandings, and mislead people, so nothing in print is allowed."

One student smiled at the thought of no books to read. His smile changed quickly when he heard the teacher say, "Every class will be a lecture from start to finish, except for the final four minutes of class, when you draw in detail a very proper picture to summarize everything you heard in class that day. The same procedure will be used in every class, every day."

Within two weeks the students really missed reading and writing. Barbara begged Ms. Jordan to change something, saying, "Ms. Jordan, it's not fair. I need words. I have ideas and opinions and questions. I can't draw all of that stuff. I can't draw my ideas the way words can describe them. Don't get me wrong, I want to behave, but I can't draw science lectures or experiments. I need to read. I need to write. I need words."

Ms. Jordan replied according to the official COP school district answer: "Words in print are prohibited. Pictures are very good and are educational. A picture is worth 1,000 words, so what you draw during this year will equal a long book."

"Ms. Jordan," Paul asked, "when we take tests to get into college, will those tests have pictures or words?" Ms. Jordan repeated the answer she had given earlier to Barbara. Ms. Jordan had to obey the laws and the school district policies.

Barbara and Paul had an idea. Words had been prohibited. The law clearly said in its audio version, which had replaced written versions of laws because words in print were prohibited, "no words in print or words in other forms that could be transformed into print." The law said nothing about individual letters. Supporters of the law were reluctant to comment that the spirit of the law included a prohibition against individual letters because opponents of the law were already saying that the letter of the law, what it exactly and clearly said, made no mention of individual letters.

The letter W began to appear throughout the school and in many places in the town. The mayor checked the law and was very frustrated. How had individual letters escaped? It was time to prohibit letters before someone started organizing letters into words.

Paul and Barbara made sure that one W was very close to a second W and to a third W whenever possible. WWW became a local curiosity. World Wide Web? No. We Want Words.

Elementary school students wore shirts with a big W on them. When three students stood together the We Want Words message was clear.

Middle school students got stickers and buttons made with a W on each. Where there were three people with buttons or stickers, the message was clear: We Want Words.

The high school marching band performed at the Friday night football game. They arranged themselves into three connecting W shapes. The crowd chanted, "We Want Words."

In a few weeks the law prohibiting words in print was repealed. Words were back; even though written words can cause conflict and confusion, they can be used in so many more good ways.

As for the name, City of Pictures, it had to be changed. The new name became Wordtown, which helped this community transform itself into a great place to live, to think, to write, and to learn.

Barbara asked the first questions in her first-period Science class the day after the printed-word prohibition was repealed. "Please, could we write something today, now? Sentences and paragraphs? Please, could we write?" Other students joined in. "Yeah, we want words. We want words."

Ms. Jordan smiled and said, "What a great idea. Please write your thoughts about why we should always allow and encourage words that people write. Add a few thoughts about why we need written words in Science, in your favorite hobby, and in real life overall."

The students eagerly wrote. This was real life. Words had been taken away from them in their real lives. Writing had been taken away from them. Pictures are good, but pictures cannot tell everything. Finally, words and writing were back, and the students expressed very convincing ideas that they put into very lively words as they wrote their essays. With this enthusiasm about written words, the future of subjects, verbs, sentences, paragraphs, ideas, and writing is one of extremely vast possibilities. Extreme writing can enhance those possibilities for words, for students, and for teachers.

# INDEX

# ABOUT THE AUTHOR

**Keen J. Babbage** has twenty-five years of experience as a teacher and administrator in middle school, high school, college, and graduate school. He is the author of *911: The School Administrator's Guide to Crisis Management* (1996), *Meetings for School-Based Decision Making* (1997), *High-Impact Teaching: Overcoming Student Apathy* (1998), *Extreme Teaching* (2002), *Extreme Learning* (2004), *Extreme Students* (2005), *Results-Driven Teaching: Teach So Well That Every Student Learns* (2006), *Extreme Economics* (first edition, 2007), *What Only Teachers Know about Education* (2008), and *Extreme Economics* (second edition, 2009), all published by Rowman & Littlefield Education.